Dawn M. Shinew, PhD
Scott Walter, MA, MLS
Editors

Information Literacy Instruction for Educators: Professional Knowledge for an Information Age

Information Literacy Instruction for Educators: Professional Knowledge for an Information Age has been co-published simultaneously as *Behavioral & Social Sciences Librarian*, Volume 22, Number 1 2003.

Pre-publication REVIEWS, COMMENTARIES, EVALUATIONS . . .

"**A**N EXCELLENT RESOURCE for any librarian or educator concerned with the information literacy skills of pre-service teachers. The contributors describe excellent examples of programs from around the world where teaching faculty and librarians are collaborating to give pre-service teachers the strategies and knowledge they need to incorporate information literacy into their own teaching. A useful annotated bibliography culls the research of librarianship and education for the most significant writings on this issue."

Jennifer Dorner, MLS
Humanities and Social Science Librarian
Portland State University

More pre-publication
REVIEWS, COMMENTARIES, EVALUATIONS . . .

"IMPORTANT. . . . Addresses the need to help future teachers demonstrate information literacy. . . . Describes the technologies that are necessary to bring the application of information literacy concepts to pre-service teachers. . . . Emphasizes the need for pre-service teachers to become fully acquainted with the potential for use of the media center to support their future classroom instruction. . . . builds a case for the importance of 'teaching teachers to teach' and why information literacy is key to effective pedagogy. . . . Lays a foundation for further discussion on how our college and university teacher training programs need to come to terms with information-age instruction–and that they need to do so very quickly."

Daniel Callison, EdD
Professor and Executive
Associate Dean,
School of Library & Information Science
Indiana University–Purdue
University at Indianapolis

"ACADEMICS AND PROFESSIONALS IN THE FIELD OF EDUCATION WILL FIND MUCH IN THIS BOOK to stimulate discussion and reflection on their own 'learning to learn' and on their ability to teach others the skills and understandings needed for 'learning to learn.' TEACHER-LIBRARIANS AND EDUCATORS OF TEACHER-LIBRARIANS WILL FIND THIS BOOK FASCINATING AS WELL. The educators referred to in the title include education librarians as well as the educators of pre-service teachers, of administrators, and of doctoral students. The contributions have been carefully selected to address three dimensions of information literacy that are critical to all educators: the information literacy skills and understandings needed by educators; the skills and understandings needed to teach information literacy skills and understandings to others; and the skills and understandings needed to work with librarians and to use library resources."

Dianne Oberg, PhD
Professor and Chair
Department of Elementary Education
University of Alberta

More pre-publication
REVIEWS, COMMENTARIES, EVALUATIONS . . .

"Shinew and Walter have brought together AN INFORMATIVE AND POWERFUL GROUP OF AUTHORS AND ESSAYS. Not only does this book provide a firm foundation for integrating information literacy into teacher education, but also and more importantly, it is a strong advocacy resource for teachers, academic and school librarians, and teacher educators. Anyone who has a vested interest in improving teacher education, student achievement, and the state of information literacy in the twenty-first century should read this book."

Stephanie Davis-Kahl, MLS
Research Librarian for Education and Outreach
University of California
Irvine Libraries

"OF SPECIAL INTEREST to those librarians and educators who are currently evaluating the place of information literacy in the curriculum for training pre-service teachers. . . . The book does an excellent job of taking the temperature of the current research and thinking regarding information literacy in the schooling of pre-service educators in the United States, Canada, and Australia."

Douglas Cook, EdD
Instruction Librarian
Shippensburg University
of Pennsylvania

The Haworth Information Press
An Imprint of The Haworth Press, Inc.

Information Literacy Instruction for Educators: Professional Knowledge for an Information Age

Information Literacy Instruction for Educators: Professional Knowledge for an Information Age has been co-published simultaneously as *Behavioral & Social Sciences Librarian*, Volume 22, Number 1 2003.

Behavioral & Social Sciences Librarian™ Monographic "Separates"

Below is a list of "separates," which in serials librarianship means a special issue simultaneously published as a special journal issue or double-issue and as a "separate" hardbound monograph. (This is a format which we also call a "DocuSerial.")

"Separates" are published because specialized libraries or professionals may wish to purchase a specific thematic issue by itself in a format which can be separately cataloged and shelved, as opposed to purchasing the journal on an on-going basis. Faculty members may also more easily consider a "separate" for classroom adoption.

"Separates" are carefully classified separately with the major book jobbers so that the journal tie-in can be noted on new book order slips to avoid duplicate purchasing.

You may wish to visit Haworth's website at . . .

http://www.HaworthPress.com

. . . to search our online catalog for complete tables of contents of these separates and related publications.

You may also call 1-800-HAWORTH (outside US/Canada: 607-722-5857), or Fax 1-800-895-0582 (outside US/Canada: 607-771-0012), or e-mail at:

docdelivery@haworthpress.com

Information Literacy Instruction for Educators: Professional Knowledge for an Information Age, edited by Dawn M. Shinew, PhD, and Scott Walter, MA, MLS (Vol. 22, No. 1, 2003). *"IMPORTANT. . . . Describes the technologies that are necessary to bring the application of information literacy concepts to pre-service teachers." (Daniel Callison, EdD, Professor and Executive Associate Dean, School of Library & Information Science, Indiana University–Purdue University at Indianapolis)*

Peace Movement Organizations and Activists in the U.S.: An Analytic Bibliography, edited by John Lofland, PhD, Victoria L. Johnson, PhD, and Pamela Kato (Vol. 10, No. 1, 1991). *"An invaluable reference for analysts of the peace movement, activists, and citizens concerned with the fate of our planet." (Sam Marullo, PhD, Assistant Professor, Georgetown University)*

Psychology and Psychiatry Serials: A Bibliographic Aid to Collection Development, compiled by the Psychology/Psychiatry Committee, Education and Behavioral Sciences Section, The Association of College and Research Libraries, The American Library Association. Chaired by Dorothy M. Persson, PhD (Vol. 9, No. 2, 1990). *"Guaranteed to be a significant help to librarians and indeed to anyone who is responsible for the selection of periodical literature in the behavioral sciences." (Insights)*

Educational and Psychological Tests in the Academic Library, edited by Rolland H. McGiverin, MSM, MSLS (Vol. 8, No. 3/4, 1990). *"Provides insight into one of the less publicized special areas of librarianship–always fascinating as they reveal the scope of the profession and its depth of knowledge in a number of unexpected fields." (Australian Library Review)*

Las Maquiladoras: Assembly and Manufacturing Plants on the United States-Mexico Border: An International Guide, edited by Martin H. Sable, PhD (Vol. 7, No. 3/4, 1989). *"An excellent introduction on the subject." (Sara De Mundo Lo, Professor of Library Administration, University of Illinois at Urbana-Champaign)*

Guide to the Writings of Pioneer Latinamericanists of the United States, by Martin H. Sable, PhD (Vol. 7, No. 1/2, 1989). *An ideal resource for researchers and scholars interested in Latin American studies, this unique and valuable guide identifies individuals born between the years 1700 and 1910 who are or were engaged in some activity concerned with Latin America in general or any of its nations or regions.*

Mexican and Mexican-American Agricultural Labor in the United States: An International Bibliography, by Martin H. Sable, PhD (Supp #1, 1987). *"An excellent guide. . . . Useful to students of ethnic studies, labor history, agricultural management, and Mexican-American affairs." (Choice)*

Industrial Espionage and Trade Secrets, edited by Martin H. Sable, PhD (Vol. 4, No. 1, 1985). *Here is a comprehensive international bibliography on the joint topic of industrial espionage-trade secrets.*

Labor, Worklife, and Industrial Relations: Sources of Information, edited by Peter B. Allison (Vol. 3, No. 3, 1984). *"An excellent contribution to labor literature in the United States. It will be invaluable to labor libraries and useful in graduate and undergraduate collections." (American Reference Books Annual)*

Information Literacy Instruction for Educators: Professional Knowledge for an Information Age

Dawn M. Shinew
Scott Walter

Information Literacy Instruction for Educators: Professional Knowledge for an Information Age has been co-published simultaneously as *Behavioral & Social Sciences Librarian*, Volume 22, Number 1 2003.

The Haworth Information Press®
An Imprint of The Haworth Press, Inc.

New York • London • Victoria (AU)
www.HaworthPress.com

Published by

The Haworth Information Press®, 10 Alice Street, Binghamton, NY 13904-1580 USA

The Haworth Information Press® is an imprint of The Haworth Press, Inc., 10 Alice Street, Binghamton, NY 13904-1580 USA.

Information Literacy Instruction for Educators: Professional Knowledge for an Information Age has been co-published simultaneously as *Behavioral & Social Sciences Librarian*, Volume 22, Number 1 2003.

Cover design by Lora Wiggins.

Library of Congress Cataloging-in-Publication Data

Information literacy instruction for educators : professional knowledge for an information age / Dawn M. Shinew, Scott Walter, editors.
    p. cm.
    "Co-published simultaneously as Behavioral & social sciences librarian, volume 22, number 1 2003."
    Includes bibliographical references and index.
    ISBN 0-7890-2072-6 (alk. paper) – ISBN 0-7890-2073-4 (pbk. : alk. paper)
    1. Education–Computer network resources. 2. Information literacy–Study and teaching. 3. Library orientation for teachers. 4. Teachers–Training of. I. Shinew, Dawn M. II. Walter, Scott, 1967- III. Behavioral & social sciences librarian.
  LB1044.87 .I53 2003
  028.7′08831–dc22
                        2003020405

6\12\08

Indexing, Abstracting & Website/Internet Coverage

This section provides you with a list of major indexing & abstracting services. That is to say, each service began covering this periodical during the year noted in the right column. Most Websites which are listed below have indicated that they will either post, disseminate, compile, archive, cite or alert their own Website users with research-based content from this work. (This list is as current as the copyright date of this publication.)

Abstracting, Website/Indexing Coverage . . . . Year When Coverage Began

- *CINAHL (Cumulative Index to Nursing & Allied Health Literature), in print, EBSCO, and SilverPlatter, Data-Star, and PaperChase. (Support materials include Subject Heading List, Database Search Guide, and instructional video.) <http://www.cinahl.com>* **1994**

- *CNPIEC Reference Guide: Chinese National Directory of Foreign Periodicals* **1995**

- *Current Cites [Digital Libraries] [Electronic Publishing] [Multimedia & Hypermedia] [Networks & Networking] [General] <http://sunsite.berkeley.edu/CurrentCites/>* . . . . *

- *Current Index to Journals in Education* **1987**

- *e-psyche, LLC <http://www.e-psyche.net>* **2002**

- *Educational Administration Abstracts (EAA)* **1991**

- *IBZ International Bibliography of Periodical Literature <http://www.saur.de>* **1997**

- *Index Guide to College Journals (core list compiled by integrating 48 indexes frequently used to support undergraduate programs in small to medium sized libraries)* **1999**

- *Index to Periodical Articles Related to Law.* **1989**

(continued)

*Exact start date to come.

(continued)

Special Bibliographic Notes related to special journal issues (separates) and indexing/abstracting:

- indexing/abstracting services in this list will also cover material in any "separate" that is co-published simultaneously with Haworth's special thematic journal issue or DocuSerial. Indexing/abstracting usually covers material at the article/chapter level.
- monographic co-editions are intended for either non-subscribers or libraries which intend to purchase a second copy for their circulating collections.
- monographic co-editions are reported to all jobbers/wholesalers/approval plans. The source journal is listed as the "series" to assist the prevention of duplicate purchasing in the same manner utilized for books-in-series.
- to facilitate user/access services all indexing/abstracting services are encouraged to utilize the co-indexing entry note indicated at the bottom of the first page of each article/chapter/contribution.
- this is intended to assist a library user of any reference tool (whether print, electronic, online, or CD-ROM) to locate the monographic version if the library has purchased this version but not a subscription to the source journal.
- individual articles/chapters in any Haworth publication are also available through the Haworth Document Delivery Service (HDDS).

Information Literacy Instruction for Educators: Professional Knowledge for an Information Age

CONTENTS

ABOUT THE EDITORS

Dawn M. Shinew, PhD, is Assistant Professor in the Department of Teaching and Learning in the Washington State University College of Education, and former coordinator of the K-8 teacher education program. She received her PhD from The Ohio State University in Social Studies and Global Education. Dr. Shinew teaches the elementary social studies methods courses, as well as graduate research courses. She is also a co-principal investigator on the Collaboration for Teacher Education Accountable to Children with High-needs (CO-TEACH) grant, a five-year Teacher Quality Enhancement grant awarded to Washington State University in 1999. As part of her role as a co-principal investigator, Dr. Shinew works in partnership with the Tacoma School District in pre-service and in-service teacher education. Her research on citizenship and gender issues have appeared in the journal *Theory and Research in Social Education* (2001) and a collection of field-based research on adolescent girls entitled *Geographies of Girlhood: Spaces In-Between* (in press).

Scott Walter, MA, MLS, is Interim Assistant Director for Public Services and Outreach at the Washington State University Libraries. Mr. Walter received his MA in Education from American University, and his MLS and his MA in History and Philosophy of Education from Indiana University. Formerly the Head of the George B. Brain Education Library and Interim Head of Library Instruction at WSU, he has also taught and supervised student teachers at the secondary level, taught at the undergraduate and graduate levels in teacher and administrator education programs at Indiana University and Washington State University, and taught in the Graduate School of Library & Information Science at the University of Illinois at Urbana-Champaign. Mr. Walter's work on education librarianship and information literacy instruction has appeared in *Education Libraries* (2001) and *Behavioral & Social Sciences Librarian* (2001), as well as in collections such as *The Collaborative Imperative: Librarians and Faculty Working Together in the Information Universe* (2000), and *A Guide to the Management of Curriculum Materials Centers for the 21st Century: The Promise and the Challenge* (2001).

Foreword

Information literacy for educators–this topic is hot!!! This topic is important!!! Read on!!!

Information Literacy Instruction for Educators: Professional Knowledge for an Information Age edited by Dawn M. Shinew and Scott Walter is a ground-breaking book, and that's why I am very pleased to write this foreword. Just a few years ago, school librarians were the only educators who were really talking about information literacy. They talked about information skills–taught in collaboration with classroom teachers and centered on real assignments–as being essential to student learning and achievement. In some schools, a few classroom teachers and administrators listened; some even acted. But, little substantive learning of information literacy really made its way into the majority of schools.

Fortunately–for our kids (and ultimately for us, because someday they are going to need these skills in order to solve the serious problems facing our world)–information literacy is starting to catch on. For one thing, educators and parents are beginning to question the mad rush to technology. Where's the impact? Where's the change in performance and achievement? Did we really invest all this money and time and effort so that kids can do PowerPoint shows? For another thing, there is a growing realization that maybe the 3 R's don't really describe the full scope of basic skills required for success in our information-rich world.

So, information literacy is beginning to work its way into the consciousness of schools and school districts. Library media specialists are often the instigators, but classroom teachers and administrators as well as parents and the community are receptive to the message or picking it up on their own: Our kids need a new skill set for the 21st century. It's not really about computers and technology–it's about "information."

[Haworth co-indexing entry note]: "Foreword." Eisenberg, Michael B. Co-published simultaneously in *Behavioral & Social Sciences Librarian* (The Haworth Information Press, an imprint of The Haworth Press, Inc.) Vol. 22, No. 1, 2003, pp. xv-xvi; and: *Information Literacy Instruction for Educators: Professional Knowledge for an Information Age* (ed: Dawn M. Shinew, and Scott Walter) The Haworth Information Press, an imprint of The Haworth Press, Inc., 2003, pp. xiii-xiv. Single or multiple copies of this article are available for a fee from The Haworth Document Delivery Service [1-800-HAWORTH, 9:00 a.m. - 5:00 p.m. (EST). E-mail address: docdelivery@haworthpress.com].

xiii

Learning in the 21st century is an exciting but challenging journey for both teachers and students. In an ever-changing technological world, there's a new literacy–information literacy–and it needs to be fully integrated into the curriculum in our schools.

It's time for teacher education programs, pre- and in-service, to get in the game. Yes, I know, "there's too much to cover already." And, I can hear the complaining, "How are we going to fit it into an already packed curriculum?" These are legitimate issues, but let's not lose sight of the goal: student success in an information-rich world requires students to become effective users of information. Information literacy is essential and important.

So, how do we develop and implement successful information literacy programs in pre-service teacher education and in-service professional development? Well, read on! Answering these questions is exactly what Dawn Shinew and Scott Walter do in this collection. There is a clear bias–each author whose work is presented in this volume starts from the premise that information literacy instruction is important across all of the programs offered to pre-service educators.

The articles in this collection are from colleges and universities where librarians, teacher educators, and administrator educators are beginning to recognize and understand the high need for integrated, authentic information literacy instruction. The examples offer useful teaching strategies and techniques on how to incorporate information literacy instruction into pre-service programs. These approaches will help teachers integrate information literacy skills into classroom learning. While each approach is unique, they all stress the importance and need for information literacy instruction in schools and colleges of education. And, the articles show, by example, how information literacy can be a meaningful part of teacher and administrator education programs.

So, to summarize, just let me repeat what I said at the beginning: Information literacy for educators–this topic is hot!!! This topic is important!!! Read on to see how information literacy can be a meaningful part of your world!!

Michael B. Eisenberg
Dean and Professor
University of Washington Information School

Information Literacy Instruction
for Educators:
A Global Perspective on Needs
and Opportunities

Scott Walter
Dawn M. Shinew

At the start of the Fall 2002 semester, the co-editors of this volume stood before a new cohort of pre-service teachers attending the first meeting of their "Teaching Elementary Social Studies" course and asked three simple questions: does anyone remember what happened in New York City on September 11, 2001?; what do you think became the most important, new part of every social studies curriculum in America on September 12th?; and, how do you think all those social studies (and other) teachers became more familiar with issues such as international terrorism, the history of the Middle East and U.S.-Arab relations, and the religion of Islam? Suddenly recognizing the ongoing need that educators have to be able to learn new things and to distinguish between fact, opinion, and rhetoric across a wide variety of topics, these pre-ser-

Scott Walter is Interim Assistant Director for Public Services and Outreach in the University Libraries, Washington State University, Pullman, WA (E-mail: swalter@wsu.edu).

Dawn M. Shinew is Assistant Professor and Coordinator of the K-8 Teacher Education Program in the College of Education, Washington State University, Pullman, WA (E-mail: dshinew@wsu.edu).

[Haworth co-indexing entry note]: "Information Literacy Instruction for Educators: A Global Perspective on Needs and Opportunities." Walter, Scott, and Dawn M. Shinew. Co-published simultaneously in *Behavioral & Social Sciences Librarian* (The Haworth Information Press, an imprint of The Haworth Press, Inc.) Vol. 22, No. 1, 2003, pp. 1-5; and: *Information Literacy Instruction for Educators: Professional Knowledge for an Information Age* (ed: Dawn M. Shinew, and Scott Walter) The Haworth Information Press, an imprint of The Haworth Press, Inc., 2003, pp. 1-5. Single or multiple copies of this article are available for a fee from The Haworth Document Delivery Service [1-800-HAWORTH, 9:00 a.m. - 5:00 p.m. (EST). E-mail address: docdelivery@haworthpress.com].

http://www.haworthpress.com/store/product.asp?sku=J103
Digital Object Identifier: 10.1300/J103v22n01_01

vice teachers were now ready to learn about how they could become more information literate.

The journey to this moment had begun almost a year earlier. In 1999, Washington State University (WSU) was awarded $9.67 million through a U.S. Department of Education Teacher Quality Enhancement grant. The project, Collaboration for Teacher Education Accountable to Children with High-needs (CO-TEACH), provided support for the co-editors' efforts in infusing information literacy throughout WSU's elementary teacher education program. The co-editors worked in collaboration with five additional faculty members who teach methods courses to revise existing assignments and focus pre-service teachers' attention to acquiring information literacy skills and applying these skills to instructional plans. These efforts reflected a shared determination that information literacy, if it is to be a meaningful part of teacher education, cannot be an "add on" to the established curriculum. Instead, information literacy must be fully integrated, and effectively modeled, throughout pre-service teachers' coursework. In developing a model to achieve this within WSU's program, the co-editors became increasingly interested in how other education programs were achieving similar objectives. This collection provides insights into journeys on which others have embarked in an effort to respond to the challenges we faced.[1]

Teacher educators and librarians have noted for decades the need for more effective information literacy instruction for our K-12 educators of tomorrow (O'Hanlon, 1988), but there have been few models of effective and programmatic approaches to information literacy instruction for educators (Carr, 1998). It has only been in recent years that a rich body of examples has arisen to guide us toward integrated, authentic information literacy instruction in schools and colleges of education. The approach to addressing this issue taken by the co-editors is rooted in the idea of "instructional outreach," i.e., a model in which academic librarians and classroom faculty collaborate to infuse information literacy instruction throughout an academic program by facilitating communication between their units and fostering faculty development in the area of information literacy instruction and assessment (Johnson, McCord, & Walter, 2003), but the essays collected in this volume bring together a wide variety of approaches to providing information literacy instruction to distinct groups of faculty and students in education programs, including pre-service teachers and teacher educators, pre-service administrators, and doctoral students preparing to become the next generation of educational leaders.

Each essay documents the need for focused attention to what the co-editors have referred to as the three dimensions of information literacy instruction for educators:

1. developing information literacy skills related to one's work as a student and as a lifelong learner (i.e., the ability to locate, evaluate, manage, and present information on a variety of topics, as needed);
2. integrating information literacy instruction into the professional skills expected of future teachers (i.e., the ability to integrate instructional objectives associated with information literacy into content-area instruction in fields such as social studies or science so that each future teacher will be able to provide information literacy instruction for his or her future students); and,
3. introducing the role of the school library as a site-based information resource, and the school librarian as a potential collaborator in the development of information skills instruction for one's future students (e.g., through integration of the school library into the round of instructional arenas commonly encountered during field experiences).

While the authors whose work is collected in this volume have taken different approaches either to articulating the need for information literacy instruction in schools and colleges of education, or to developing models for integrating information literacy instruction into the pre-service teacher and administrator education curriculum, there are several overlapping themes that are reinforced in a number of these programs.

First, there is a recognition that existing teacher and administrator education programs continue to neglect information literacy instruction as a programmatic element of the curriculum despite the attention paid to this very issue in national reports such as the Association of College & Research Libraries' *Progress Report on Information Literacy* (1998), and the final report of the American Association of School Librarians/Association of College & Research Libraries Task Force on the Educational Role of Libraries, *Blueprint for Collaboration* (2000). This issue has been addressed in earlier works, including that of Carr (1998), Wilson and Blake (1993), Wilson and McNeill (1998), and Asselin and Lee (2002), but it is powerfully reinforced by Asselin and Doiron, whose study of Canadian teacher education faculty members' perception of the profession's neglect of information literacy instruction is included in this collection.

Also evident in this collection is the importance of information literacy instruction across all of the programs offered to pre-service educators. Hinchliffe establishes the context for developing a concept of information literacy in light of technological developments. Johnson and O'English provide an annotated bibliography for this collection that identifies several studies of information literacy instruction for pre-service teachers, but articles by Roberson, Schweinle, and Applin on pre-service administrators, and by Grant and Berg on doctoral students, reflect a broader focus. The information literacy instruction that one offers to a pre-service teacher will share certain elements with that offered to a pre-service administrator, but there are also distinctions that are derived from the different roles that these future educators will play in our school system. Each article in this collection provides practical ideas for identifying instructional needs among an identifiable group of learners in a school or college of education; together, they provide an effective framework for working across the diversified curriculum of pre-service education.

Finally, this collection demonstrates the universal nature of the need to provide more effective information literacy instruction for pre-service educators. The case studies of teacher education programs in the United States (Witt and Dickinson), Canada (Branch), and Australia (Lipu) represent a unique attempt to illustrate effective practices in information literacy instruction for educators from around the world. As importantly, the contributors are almost evenly divided between information professionals and teacher and administrator educators. Information literacy instruction is, thus, no longer seen as a "library" issue, but as an issue of significance to anyone interested in preparing educators to be reflective practitioners in an Information Age.

No collection of this size could hope to fully represent the range of activities currently being undertaken by our colleagues from around the world, but it provides a global perspective on an increasingly significant issue, i.e., how to assure that pre-service educators are provided with an authentic and effective introduction to information literacy skills that addresses their future needs not only as students, but as teachers, administrators, and lifelong learners? A future collection might address the many ways in which in-service educators are being introduced to the idea of information literacy and to the instructional methods best suited to fostering information literacy among the rising generation (e.g., Nichols, 1999). We hope that an introduction to the issues addressed in this collection and to the exemplary programs described herein in brief will provide you with a road-map for facilitating similar activities on your own campuses, or in your own communities and schools.

NOTE

1. For more information in the CO-TEACH project, please visit the project Web site at <http://www.educ.wsu.edu/coe/coteach/newsite/index.html>.

REFERENCES

AASL/ACRL Task Force on the Educational Role of Libraries. 2000. *Blueprint for collaboration* [online]. Chicago: Association of College & Research Libraries [cited 5 March 2003]. Available World Wide Web <http://www.ala.org/acrl/blueprint.html>.

Asselin, Marlene, and Elizabeth A. Lee. 2002. "I wish someone had taught me": Information literacy in a teacher education program. *Teacher Librarian* 30: 10-17.

Association of College & Research Libraries. 1998. *A progress report on information literacy: An update on the American Library Association Presidential Committee on Information Literacy: Final report* [online]. Chicago: The Author [cited 5 March 2003]. Available World Wide Web <http://www.ala.org/acrl/nili/nili.html>.

Carr, Jo Ann. 1998. *Information literacy and teacher education* [online]. Washington, DC: ERIC Clearinghouse on Teaching and Teacher Education. (ERIC Document Reproduction Service No. ED 424231) [cited 5 March 2003]. Available World Wide Web <http://www.ericfacility.net/ericdigests/ed424231.html>.

Johnson, Corey M., Sarah K. McCord, and Scott Walter. 2003. Instructional outreach across the curriculum: Enhancing the liaison role at a research university. *The Reference Librarian* 82: 19-37.

Nichols, Janet. 1999. Building bridges: High school and university partnerships for information literacy. *NASSP Bulletin* 83 (no. 605): 75-81.

O'Hanlon, Nancy. 1988. Up the down staircase: Establishing library instruction programs for teachers. *RQ* 27: 528-34.

Wilson, Patricia, and Martha Blake. 1993. The missing piece: A school library media center component in principal preparation programs. *Record in Educational Administration and Supervision* 13 (2): 65-68.

Wilson, Patricia, and Angus McNeill. 1998. In the dark: What's keeping principals from understanding libraries? *School Library Journal* 44 (9): 114-116.

Technology and the Concept
of Information Literacy
for Pre-Service Teachers

Lisa Janicke Hinchliffe

SUMMARY. Through an examination of a variety of information literacy documents and an analysis of supporting materials, the author argues that the impact of technology on the conceptualization of information is two-fold: technology serves as a catalyst for developing a rationale for the importance of the concept and as a mechanism for focusing attention on specific issues within the broader concept of information literacy. Though the discussion is contextualized within the field of education, the majority of the ideas raised apply to information literacy for any discipline or profession. The chapter ends with a discussion of additional considerations related to information literacy and digital technologies within the field of education. *[Article copies available for a fee from The Haworth Document Delivery Service: 1-800-HAWORTH. E-mail address: <docdelivery@haworthpress.com> Website: <http://www.HaworthPress.com> © 2003 by The Haworth Press, Inc. All rights reserved.]*

KEYWORDS. Information literacy, technology literacy, teacher education

Through an examination of a variety of information literacy documents and an analysis of supporting materials, this article argues that

Lisa Janicke Hinchliffe is Associate Professor of Library Administration and Coordinator for Information Literacy Services and Instruction, University of Illinois at Urbana-Champaign, Urbana, IL (E-mail: ljanicke@uiuc.edu).

[Haworth co-indexing entry note]: "Technology and the Concept of Information Literacy for Pre-Service Teachers." Hinchliffe, Lisa Janicke. Co-published simultaneously in *Behavioral & Social Sciences Librarian* (The Haworth Information Press, an imprint of The Haworth Press, Inc.) Vol. 22, No. 1, 2003, pp. 7-18; and: *Information Literacy Instruction for Educators: Professional Knowledge for an Information Age* (ed: Dawn M. Shinew, and Scott Walter) The Haworth Information Press, an imprint of The Haworth Press, Inc., 2003, pp. 7-18. Single or multiple copies of this article are available for a fee from The Haworth Document Delivery Service [1-800-HAWORTH, 9:00 a.m. - 5:00 p.m. (EST). E-mail address: docdelivery@haworthpress.com].

http://www.haworthpress.com/store/product.asp?sku=J103
© 2003 by The Haworth Press, Inc. All rights reserved.
Digital Object Identifier: 10.1300/J103v22n01_02

7

the impact of technology on the conceptualization of information literacy is two-fold: technology serves as a catalyst for developing a rationale for the importance of the concept and as a mechanism for focusing attention on specific issues within the broader concept of information literacy. Understanding the relationship between technology and information literacy is particularly important in light of recent findings from the Pew Internet and American Life Project (2002) that "many schools and teachers have not yet recognized–much less responded to–the new ways students communicate and access information over the Internet" (iii), resulting in a "digital disconnect" (v) between students and teachers with respect to Internet-based information seeking. The discussion is thus contextualized within the field of education, but the majority of the ideas raised here apply to information literacy for any discipline or profession. The article ends with a discussion of additional considerations related to information literacy and digital technologies within the field of education.

THE CONCEPTUALIZATION OF INFORMATION LITERACY

Writing about the impact of technology on information literacy and library instruction has many challenges, not the least of which is determining what is meant by "information literacy." Perhaps the most often quoted definition of information literacy was articulated in the *Final Report of the American Library Association Presidential Committee on Information Literacy* (1989):

> To be information literate, a person must be able to recognize when information is needed and have the ability to locate, evaluate, and use effectively the needed information . . . Ultimately, information literate people are those who have learned how to learn. They know how to learn because they know how knowledge is organized, how to find information, and how to use information in such a way that others can learn from them.

This narrative definition is echoed in most writing on information literacy since 1989 and is the foundation of the *Information Literacy Competency Standards for Higher Education* (2000). Indeed, the influence of this definition is particularly obvious in the structure of the *Standards*, which delineates one standard for each of the four general characteristics (identify needs, locate, evaluate, and use) plus a fifth to address the issues of legality, ethics, and social environment that attend to the exercise of information literacy. As such, though some might take issue with this definition from the *Final Report*, it stands as the touchstone document for the library profession and, in some ways, functions as a benchmark against which other definitions of information literacy are judged.

IMPACT OF TECHNOLOGY ON INFORMATION LITERACY

Thinking about the relationship between information literacy and technology, it is interesting to note that the very first paragraph of the *Final Report* points to technology as a source of the challenges faced in the information age:

> No other change in American society has offered greater challenges than the emergence of the Information Age. Information is expanding at an unprecedented rate, and enormously rapid strides are being made in the technology for storing, organizing, and accessing the ever growing tidal wave of information.

Of course, the years since this publication have seen the ever-increasing development of technology, an explosion of information resources, and the resulting disintermediation of access to information brought about through and because of technological advances.

In reflecting on the *Final Report*, the 1987 *Model Statement of Objectives for Academic Bibliographic Instruction*, and the development of information literacy as a concept, one can cautiously conclude that the developments in technology have served as a catalyst for crystallizing the concept of information literacy and the importance of information literacy for learning and civic life. Likewise, as evidenced by the Pew (2002) study, advances in technology and access to information have led to changes in the professional skills required of K-12 educators. Prior to the infusion of technology into libraries, primarily through the automation of the card catalog, publications about information literacy were very limited in number. This is no longer the case today as publications about information literacy abound. In 2000, the influence of technology on the concept of information literacy was significant enough to warrant a section in the introduction to the *Information Literacy Competency Standards for Higher Education* which serves to distinguish information literacy from information technology or computer literacy.

Beyond these general observations, in order to examine the full impact of technology on the concept of information literacy, it is useful to consider the specifics of the *Information Literacy Competency Standards for Higher Education* and the contemporary discussion of 21st century literacies.

TECHNOLOGY AND STANDARDS

As mentioned above, the introduction to the *Information Literacy Competency Standards for Higher Education* distinguishes between information literacy, computer literacy, and fluency with information technology. In doing so, the *Standards* draw on the National Research Council (1999) report, *Being Fluent with Information Technology*. The complex interplay between information literacy and information technology literacy is revealed in the identification of information literacy as "a distinct and broader area of competence" which "initiates, sustains, and extends lifelong learning through abilities which may use technologies but are ultimately independent of them" though the text also recognizes that "information literate individuals necessarily develop some technology skills." The linkage between information literacy and information technology literacy is even more apparent in the consideration of specific performance indicators and learning outcomes. The following selections exemplify this point:

> 1.1.1 Confers with instructors and participates in class discussions, peer workgroups, and electronic discussions to identify a research topic, or other information need.

> 2.2.5 Implements the search strategy in various information retrieval systems using different user interfaces and search engines, with different command languages, protocols, and search parameters.

> 2.3 The information literate student retrieves information online or in person using a variety of methods.

> 5.1. The information literate student understands many of the ethical, legal and socio-economic issues surrounding information and information technology.

Clearly, the technological tools through which information is accessed, retrieved, and manipulated are not easily separated from the information itself. Indeed, such separation would likely not be desirable since the result would not accurately represent the real-world tasks and circumstances that learners must learn to negotiate.

Moreover, in addition to the outcomes related specifically to information technology literacy, a second point is relevant to this discussion of information literacy and technology. Technology is not only part of the content of information literacy. Technology has also caused librarians, and faculty, to focus their attention on certain outcomes which do not relate to technology per se. This re-focusing is necessitated by technological changes in information access and manipulation. The most obvious example of this is the focus that is now regularly placed on evaluating information sources. Another general example is the increasing challenge of plagiarism from online resources and the need to emphasize ethical and legal use of information resources. It is important, however, not to confuse the shift in emphasis *within* the range of issues encompassed by information literacy with a shift *away from* information literacy to technological literacy per se.

21ST CENTURY LITERACIES

The final issue worth exploring with respect to technology and the conceptualization of information literacy is the notion of 21st century literacies. Nancy Kranich (2000) discussed this concept in an *American Libraries* column during her year as President of the American Library Association. In her column, "Building Partnerships for 21st-Century Literacy," Kranich presents an expanded notion of literacy for the 21st century, stating that:

> In the 21st century literacy takes on a new and expanded meaning. Information literacy means being information smart. It means knowing when a book may be more helpful than a computer. It means knowing how to make critical judgments about information: its completeness, accuracy, viewpoint. Information literacy is a critical life skill in today's information jungle.

In this representation, 21st century literacy is equivalent to information literacy.

Other authors, however, have expanded the scope of the discussion to a broader conception of contemporary literacy, which incorporates information literacy but includes other elements as well. For example, the *White Paper* (2002) from the 21st Century Literacy Summit identifies four literacies as key components of 21st century literacy:

* technology literacy
* information literacy
* media creativity
* social competence and responsibility.

The *White Paper* argues that the education, workplace, and public sectors are all stakeholders that are challenged to address 21st century literacy at individual, organizational, and societal levels. The models highlighted in the *White Paper*, the great variety of efforts underway to address the digital divide, documented, for example, at <http://www.digitaldividenetwork.org>, and the general awareness of issues related to the vast amount of information in today's society are all part of the larger context in which academic librarians pursue information literacy programming. Lipu (2003) provides another example of professional discussion of this issue in her identification of "tertiary literacies" for Australian higher education.

INFORMATION LITERACY IN THE FIELD OF EDUCATION

Before concluding this discussion of the impact of technology on information literacy as a concept, it is worth spending a little time on the "Information Retrieval and Evaluation Skills for Education Students" (1992). This statement of skills is based on the *Model Statement of Objectives for Academic Bibliographic Instruction* (1987) and its development was also motivated, in part, by changing technologies. In particular, Goal 1, Objective C states that: "The learner realizes the effects of evolving information technologies on the generation, communication, and access of information." The integration of technology into the skills expected for education students is even more apparent when one considers the specific examples of how the skills statement might be utilized for different instructional situations. The discussions of these situations mention particular technologies, primarily CD-ROM, though print resources are still very much present in the discussions.

The "Information Retrieval and Evaluation Skills for Education Students" document from the Education and Behavioral Sciences Section of the Association of College and Research Libraries is currently undergoing revision in light of the *Information Literacy Competency Standards for Higher Education*. In the revision, there will be "particular focus on the information competencies themselves and the role of the librarian in collaborating and facilitating student achievement of these competencies will be stressed."[1] Given that the revision is not complete, it is difficult to predict how technology will be integrated into the revised document; however, it seems fairly safe to suggest that the integration will likely parallel the approach taken in the *Information Literacy Competency Standards for Higher Education*.

The other document of note for considering information literacy in the field of education is the *Professional Standards for the Accreditation of Schools, Colleges, and Departments of Education* (2002). These accreditation standards are promulgated by the National Council for Accreditation of Teacher Education (NCATE), which is "the accrediting body for colleges and universities that prepare teachers and other professional personnel for work in elementary and secondary schools" (1). The American Library Association is a member organization of NCATE as are the Association for Educational Communications and Technology and the International Society for Technology in Education.

Because of the importance of NCATE accreditation for teacher education programs, the language of the accrediting standards is influential in affecting the initiatives pursued by education programs. Standard One identifies candidate knowledge, skills, and dispositions "necessary to help all students learn" (*Professional Standards*, 2002, 14) and includes a target outcome that teacher candidates "present the content to students in challenging, clear, and compelling ways and integrate technology appropriately" (15). Though information literacy is arguably implicit in the target outcomes, it is not until the supporting explanation for the standard that the concept appears explicitly:

> They are able to appropriately and effectively integrate technology and information literacy in instruction to support student learning. (19)

Though librarians would probably argue that the complementary concept of information literacy would have been better included in the target outcome language per se, the inclusion of the phrase "information literacy" in the accreditation document will likely prove useful to librarians in arguing the importance of information literacy for education students. The low-profile mention may not be notable enough to leverage as much influence as librarians would wish and so continued advocacy within the education profession is no doubt needed to bring the concept of information literacy into the foreground of the accrediting standards document.

Of course, none of this discussion is intended to diminish the importance of technology literacy for teachers as delineated in the *ISTE National Educational Technology Standards (NETS) and Performance Indicators for Teachers* by the International Society for Technology in Education (2000). Rather, because information literacy and technology literacy are easily confused, efforts here are intended to clarify their distinct yet complementary competencies in light of the complexities of pursuing information literacy and technology literacy competencies for pre-service teachers. Just as technology has influenced information literacy, so too do changes in information affect the conceptualization of technology literacy and its importance for teachers.

EDUCATION STUDENTS AS FUTURE INFORMATION LITERACY INSTRUCTORS

Finally, because much of the focus within the field of education is, rightly so, on pre-service teachers, some attention must also be paid to the information literacy standards utilized in primary and secondary school settings to which the students may find themselves accountable during student and post-baccalaureate teaching experiences. Byerly and Brodie (1999) provide an excellent summary of the many information literacy models which have been developed and implemented in primary and secondary settings throughout various parts of the United States. Though the limitations of this article do not permit a thorough consideration of the various models, a few general comments are in order.

As future teachers, pre-service education students need to be prepared to develop instruction to help their students attain information literacy learning outcomes. The challenge in preparing pre-service teachers for this role is similar to the challenge of preparing pre-service teachers with respect to other outcomes they must address in their teaching–pre-service teachers are often learning both the content to be taught as well as methods to teach it while they are in college. As Carr (1998) so clearly stated, "Teachers cannot prepare their students to be information literate unless they themselves understand how to find and use information." Thus, because pre-service teachers must be information literate as college students, but also need to be taught how to incorporate information literacy in lesson plans and curriculum development, librarians providing instruction to pre-service teachers will find that they must not only provide instruction in information literacy skills, but must also model pedagogical approaches and practices which students can then utilize in their own teaching plans.

The circumstances for the education librarian are made more complex because of the current lack of articulation between the K-12 and higher education information literacy standards. Cahoy (2002) provides a detailed comparative analysis of the *Information Literacy Competency Standards for Higher Education* and the K-12 *Information Literacy Standards for Student Learning,* pointing out that "when compared, each set of standards communicates a slightly different vision of what information literacy is and how it can be achieved by every student" (13). As such, though the two sets of standards overlap in many areas, the librarian who designs instruction for pre-service teachers based on the higher education standards may find it difficult to also provide a model of information literacy as envisioned in the K-12 standards.

Future developments may ameliorate these difficulties as a joint AASL/ACRL Information Literacy Task Force is currently charged with "pursuing writing a joint publication . . . enumerating a seamless K-20 process that reflects the Information Literacy Standards previously published by each division."[2] This future document should assist education librarians in developing instruction that both develops pre-service teachers' information literacy skills and models appropriate methods for teaching information literacy.

RELATED ISSUES

In addition to the issues related to the impact of technology on the conceptualization of information literacy as discussed above, there are many other issues related to information literacy programming for education students which deserve mention even though they cannot be addressed in full.

As is true of much of the literature within education librarianship, this article focused primarily on the information literacy needs of undergraduate students who are or who intend to become pre-service teachers. Other undergraduate and graduate programs are also likely to be found among the programs offered by a department or college of education including school counseling, student life and development, school administration, and possibly even library science, media services, and/or educational technology. For pre-service teachers, librarians might also consider whether students are prepared for the transition from the relatively information resource-rich academic library environment to the arguably significantly different school practitioner environment and, if they are not, how to best address this issue.

Also implied in the discussion of the NCATE standards, though not explicitly discussed, is the reality that education faculty members, supervising teachers, and support staff, as well as librarians, are jointly responsible for helping education students develop information literacy. The challenges and opportunities of collaboration are many but, again, can only be hinted at here with a recommendation to pursue this topic in *The Collaborative Imperative*, edited by Raspa and Ward (2000).

Related to collaboration are issues of instruction program management and administration. Education librarians are challenged to create instruction programs that are institutionalized–rather than dependent on the efforts of individual people only, systematic–rather than happenstance, and sustainable–rather than a series of pilot projects which cannot scale to reach all intended students. Theoretical frameworks relating to technological change and innovation can also be used to more carefully understand the management of instruction programs in libraries (Woodard and Hinchliffe, 2002) in addition to information literacy per se as this article addressed.

As stated, it is not possible to fully address these topics within this chapter, but they are mentioned to provide at least a cursory overview of the instructional and organizational context in which education librarians pursue information literacy instruction.

CONCLUSION

The concepts of information literacy and information literacy instruction are, as demonstrated by this discussion, complex and multi-faceted. This article focused on the conceptualization of information literacy–both generally and within the field of education, with particular attention to the complexity of the issues for pre-service teachers. With respect to conceptualizing information literacy, the impact of technology appears two-fold: as a catalyst for developing a rationale for the importance of the concept and as a mechanism for focusing attention on specific issues within the broader concept of information literacy. For librarians serving education students, the challenge of designing instruction programs is further complicated by the fact that pre-service teachers are future teachers of information literacy. Hopefully the issues discussed herein provide an overview of the impact of technology on information literacy and instruction and a useful vantage point from which to consider future developments in this arena.

NOTES

1. From http://www.lib.msu.edu/corby/ebss/02midwinter.htm#insted.
2. http://www.ala.org/assl/committees.html.

REFERENCES

Byerly, Greg and Carolyn S. Brodie. 1999. Information literacy skills models: Defining the choices. In B.K. Stripling (Ed.), *Learning and libraries in an information age: Principles and practice* (pp. 54-82). Englewood, CO: Libraries Unlimited.

Cahoy, Ellysa Stern. 2002. Will your students be ready for college? Connecting K-12 and college standards for information literacy. *Knowledge Quest*, 30(4): 12-15.

Carr, Jo Ann. 1998. *Information literacy and teacher education* [online]. Washington, DC: ERIC Clearinghouse on Teaching and Teacher Education. (ERIC Document Reproduction Service No. ED 424231) [cited 13 March 2003]. Available from World Wide Web: <http://www.ericfacility.net/ericdigests/ed424231.html>.

Final report of the American Library Association Presidential Committee on Information Literacy [online]. 1989. Chicago: American Library Association [cited 13 March 2003]. Available from World Wide Web: <http://www.ala.org/acrl/nili/ilit1st.html>.

Information literacy competency standards for higher education [online]. 2000. Chicago: Association of College and Research Libraries. [cited 13 March 2003]. Available from World Wide Web: <http://www.ala.org/acrl/ilcomstan.html>.

Information literacy standards for student learning [online]. 1998. Chicago: American Association of School Librarians and Association for Educational Communications and Technology [cited 13 March 2003]. Available from World Wide Web: <http://www.ala.org/aasl/ip_nine.html>.

Information retrieval and evaluation skills for education students. 1992. *C&RL News* 53(9): 583-588.

International Society for Technology in Education. 2000. *ISTE National Educational Technology Standards (NETS) and Performance Indicators for Teachers* [online]. Eugene, OR: International Society for Technology in Education [cited 13 March 2003]. Available from World Wide Web: <http://cnets.iste.org/teachers/pdf/page09.pdf>.

Kranich, Nancy. 2000. Building partnerships for 21st-century literacy [online]. *American Libraries* 31, no. 8 (September): 7 [cited 13 March 2003]. Available from World Wide Web: <http://www.ala.org/kranich/alcol.html#sept>.

Lipu, Suzanne. (2003). A flying start for our future teachers: A comprehensive information literacy program for pre-service education students at the University of Wollongong, Australia. *Behavioral & Social Sciences Librarian*, 22(1): 47-73.

Model statement of objectives for academic bibliographic instruction [online]. 1987. Chicago: Association of College and Research Libraries, Instruction Section [cited 13 March 2003]. Available from World Wide Web: <http://www.ala.org/acrl/guides/msobi.html>.

National Research Council. Commission on Physical Sciences, Mathematics, and Applications. Committee on Information Technology Literacy, Computer Science and Telecommunications Board. (1999). *Being fluent with information technology* [online]. Washington, D.C.: National Academy Press [cited 13 March 2003]. Available from World Wide Web: <http://www.nap.edu/catalog/6482.html>.

Pew Internet and American Life Project. 2002. *The digital disconnect: The widening gap between Internet-savvy students and their schools* [online]. Washington, DC: Pew Internet and American Life Project [cited 13 March 2003]. Available from World Wide Web: <http://www.pewinternet.org/reports/pdfs/PIP_Schools_Internet_Report.pdf>.

Professional standards for the accreditation of schools, colleges, and departments of education [online]. 2002. Washington, DC: National Council for Accreditation of Teacher Education [cited 13 March 2003]. Available from World Wide Web: <http://www.ncate.org/2000/unit_stnds_2002.pdf>.

Raspa, Dick, and Dane Ward, Eds. 2000. *The collaborative imperative: Librarians and faculty working together in the information universe.* Chicago: Association of College and Research Libraries.

White paper: 21st century literacy in a convergent media world [online]. 2002. Berlin: 21st Century Literacy Summit [cited 13 March 2003]. Available from World Wide Web: <http://www.21stcenturyliteracy.org/white/WhitePaperEnglish.pdf>.

Woodard, Beth S., and Lisa Janicke Hinchliffe. 2002. Technology and innovation in library instruction management. *Journal of Library Administration* 36(1/2): 39-55.

Whither They Go:
An Analysis of the Inclusion
of School Library Programs and Services
in the Preparation of Pre-Service Teachers
in Canadian Universities

Marlene Asselin
Ray Doiron

SUMMARY. This study investigated how teacher education programs address the role of school libraries in supporting current educational and curriculum reform, especially integrated information literacy instruction. Methods instructors, practicum coordinators, and library staff from a stratified random sample of 17 teacher education programs in Canada were surveyed and interviewed. While results indicated that teacher educators value the role of school libraries in teaching and learning, pre-service teachers are not effectively learning about school library programs and

Marlene Asselin is Assistant Professor, Department of Language and Literacy Education, University of British Columbia, Canada, and coordinator of the teacher-librarian education program, Vancouver, BC, Canada (E-mail: marlene.asselin@ubc.ca).

Ray Doiron is Associate Professor, Faculty of Education, University of Prince Edward Island, Canada (E-mail: raydoiron@upei.ca).

[Haworth co-indexing entry note]: "Whither They Go: An Analysis of the Inclusion of School Library Programs and Services in the Preparation of Pre-Service Teachers in Canadian Universities." Asselin, Marlene, and Ray Doiron. Co-published simultaneously in *Behavioral & Social Sciences Librarian* (The Haworth Information Press, an imprint of The Haworth Press, Inc.) Vol. 22, No. 1, 2003, pp. 19-32; and: *Information Literacy Instruction for Educators: Professional Knowledge for an Information Age* (ed: Dawn M. Shinew, and Scott Walter) The Haworth Information Press, an imprint of The Haworth Press, Inc., 2003, pp. 19-32. Single or multiple copies of this article are available for a fee from The Haworth Document Delivery Service [1-800-HAWORTH, 9:00 a.m. - 5:00 p.m. (EST). E-mail address: docdelivery@haworthpress.com].

Digital Object Identifier: 10.1300/J103v22n01_03

services and information literacy pedagogy. Evidence-based implications for advocacy initiatives in teacher education programs are offered. *[Article copies available for a fee from The Haworth Document Delivery Service: 1-800-HAWORTH. E-mail address: <docdelivery@haworthpress.com> Website: <http://www.HaworthPress.com> © 2003 by The Haworth Press, Inc. All rights reserved.]*

KEYWORDS. Information literacy, teacher education, school libraries, field experiences

Current trends in educational and curriculum reform indicate an increasingly strong role for information literacy yet it is not known if information literacy is being integrated into pre-service teacher education. Recent policy documents in school librarianship identify information literacy as a major focus in school library programs (American Association of School Librarians and the Association for Educational Communications and Technology, 1998; Association for Teacher-librarianship in Canada and the Canadian School Library Association, 1997). In Canada, national agencies view education as "a lifelong learning process and (educators must) strive to create a learning society in which the acquisition, renewal, and use of knowledge are cherished" (Council of Ministers of Education, 1999). Proponents of media literacy also embed information literacy in their policy and curriculum documents (Media Awareness Network, 2002). Such vision statements imply that information literacy is the concern of all educators and one of the principal expectations society has for future citizens. Current learning outcomes (Western and Northern Canadian Protocol, 2003) and standards for information literacy (American Association of School Librarians and the Association for Educational Communications and Technology 1998; National Council of Teachers of English and the International Reading Association, 1996; International Society for Technology Education, 2000-2002) provide educators with clear directions in today's classrooms. While professional organizations and some higher education institutions have recognized the need to include information literacy in the development of pre-service teachers, Carr (1998) reports that this integration has not taken place widely, in spite of there being several models for such integration that have worked well in some teacher preparation programs (Asselin & Lee, 2002).

In response to broader educational and curricular reform movements, teacher education programs have been going through a general renewal (Shapson, 1998). Hargreaves' (1995) landmark study examined teacher education reform and recognized factors like decentralization, "work intensification" and global cultural change as important ones that are changing teacher education. As in the United States (National Commission on Teaching and America's Future, 1996), Hargreaves called for the "restructuring of teaching" to address issues around accountability and differentiated roles for teachers, as well as a major redesign of curriculum and instruction which will promote and develop higher-order thinking skills.

While the emergence of information literacy as a major force in educational reform and the concurrent changes in teacher education have been significant, there has been an overall drop in the number of faculty in school library education and in the number of school library programs. Although there are no published records of numbers of accredited programs in Canada, during the 1980s there were programs in almost every province. There are still some courses offered in isolated spots in the country, but unless the Faculty offers a Diploma Program in School Librarianship, a Master's of Education in librarianship or a few in-service courses for summer students, most new teachers appear to receive little training or even exposure to the role that the teacher-librarian plays in developing an information literacy curriculum in partnership with classroom teachers. It could be that the traditional attention paid to the role of the school library and to its instructional program when spearheaded by a teacher-librarian may have been subsumed under other courses, but there was no evidence to support that assumption. To clarify the situation, an investigation of school library education within the pre-service programs of Canada's universities was undertaken with the hope that accurate information on what is happening in Faculties of Education would lead to new efforts to improve the situation. Without a new generation of teachers knowledgeable about school libraries, how teacher-librarians support the development of information literacy, how school libraries pass on our cultural heritage, how information technologies help us learn, and how school libraries act as community access points for teachers and students, it will be impossible for schools to have fully integrated school library programs in the future.

To investigate this sense of a diminished presence for school librarianship in most pre-service programs in Canadian universities, we conducted a national study on pre-service teacher preparation. The focus was on how new teachers are being prepared to understand the role of school libraries in today's schools and how they learn to provide information literacy instruction. Three objectives guided the investigation:

- to examine the extent and character of the erosion of school library education in Canadian Faculties of Education;
- to identify alternatives that Faculties of Education may have found for including the role of the school library in pre-service programs; and
- to identify if and how Faculties of Education prepare pre-service educators for their role of developing information literate citizens.

METHODOLOGY

The research was conducted with a representative sample of Faculties of Education from across Canada. A stratified random sample of 17 teacher education programs from all regions of Canada was identified. The sample represented large programs (over 500 students), medium-sized programs (200-499 students) and small programs (less than 200 students). Data collection was based on a questionnaire and telephone interviews to extend the questionnaire data. For each institution, questionnaires were sent to the coordinators of the literacy and social studies methods courses, the practicum coordinator, and a library staff person with major responsibilities in the Faculty of Education. We received responses from 94% of the programs selected for survey, with 38% (n = 26) of individuals surveyed completing a questionnaire. Telephone interviews lasting 30 minutes were conducted with nine volunteers drawn from those who had completed a questionnaire. For each of the three research objectives, data analysis utilized descriptive statistics and the constant-comparative method for identifying themes in questionnaire responses and telephone interviews.

RESULTS

The results are organized around the three main research objectives and reported as summary charts from the questionnaires and recurring themes identified in the interviews.

Extent and Character of the Erosion of School Library Education in Canadian Faculties of Education

Questionnaire respondents rated the importance of five different roles for the teacher-librarian in achieving the learning outcomes of today's curriculum. Table 1 reports mean ratings of the five roles on a scale of 1-5.

TABLE 1. Teacher Educators' Ascribed Importance of the Role of the Teacher-Librarian in Achieving Curriculum Outcomes

Teacher-librarian role	Importance
Collaborate with teachers	4.72
Teach information skills	4.59
Promote reading and lifelong learning	4.56
Provide wide range of resources	4.50
Use information technology for learning	4.50

While teacher education faculty appear to highly value the role of the teacher-librarian in the broader educational context, other analyses indicated an absence of larger programmatic structures to support pre-service teachers' understanding of the relationship between school library programs and services to prescribed curriculum. Specifically, our analysis revealed the following major structural indicators of a diminished role for school library education in pre-service education programs:

1. Relevant courses are still on books but have not been offered for several years.
2. Faculty members in the school library have moved to other responsibilities or retired.
3. Practicum placements in school libraries are rare.
4. Role of school library is not explicitly part of teacher education.
5. Information literacy skills and pedagogy are not explicitly or systemically part of teacher education.

Discussions held with the telephone interviewees confirmed the questionnaire findings and added more evidence of the deterioration of school library education in Canadian Faculties of Education. Many interviewees expressed alarm and concern about the erosion of any visible role for school libraries. They saw a "deterioration in the values associated with libraries," and recognized a need for all teacher educators to "step up here and start telling people we are losing something very important." One interviewee said, "The conditions are worsening and no one is trying to stop it." Several saw that "school library collections are languishing as instructional tools," while "the feeling of going to the library is lost."

Interviewees described examples of information literacy related projects students did as part of their coursework, but each person admitted these projects were never completed within the context of the role of school libraries in achieving various information literacy outcomes. "No one is explicitly or deliberately doing anything related to information literacy or the role of school libraries. It is perhaps mentioned here and there, but not with any focus or vision." Throughout the interviews, there was a very strong feeling that "we have not even thought of the school library; we assume someone else is doing it, but it is not being done."

In a similar way, the skills associated with information literacy such as working with the research process are very much a part of revitalized methods courses, but little is done to show pre-service teachers how to develop these skills with their future students. "It is assumed that students will learn these skills by doing the projects that are assigned to them." Course instructors and library staff who were interviewed referred to how a wide range of learning resources are being used by professors and students for course assignments and students' lesson planning. In some cases, students are expected to apply critical thinking skills, but only in their selection of appropriate resources or to filter Internet Web sites. In most cases, "the push is on to use a diverse set of resources by students in their programs, but even then the school library as a source of these materials is basically ignored."

Comments were made about how the role of school libraries is never discussed at faculty meetings nor is anyone taking a leadership role in building it into the pre-service experience of new teachers. "Lack of information is a real problem since faculty and students do not really understand the role of the school library and the role of the teacher-librarian." Several even went so far as to suggest that "faculties of education have slipped in their responsibilities here and they need to be made aware of that and brought to task on it."

Practice teaching placements in school libraries appeared to be rare to the point of being nonexistent. Only one interviewee had any examples of pre-service teachers being placed in a school library for their practicum, while it was more common for people to react by saying, "no placements are being done in the school library; the students are allowed to do them, but it is not even mentioned as an option." One interviewee summed it up bluntly: "A student teacher could go into a school and teach for the whole practicum and get a pass without ever having gone to the school library." Cuts to teacher-librarian positions across the country have made it less likely for such placements to occur even if teacher education programs took up this initiative.

To those working in school library education, these findings come as no surprise. However, the bold recognition of these circumstances by "outsiders" and their comments around these facts serve as a wake-up call and provide a springboard for action.

Alternatives for Including the Role of the School Library in Pre-Service Programs

If school libraries and the role of the teacher-librarian are not being developed explicitly through the traditional methods of specific courses and leadership from a particular faculty member, our second question was aimed at identifying alternative ways that may have emerged for including these areas in pre-service education. Table 2 summarizes the questionnaire data on methods used by faculty to introduce new teachers to the school library.

All of the items listed in Table 2 are examples taken from specific courses and practicum experiences and suggest that if the role of the school library is included at all, it is only in isolated events where a guest speaker or visitor gives a presentation on the role, suggesting limited integration with regular course content. In a few cases, instructors hold class discussions on the role of the school library and share information in a pamphlet or lecture. Less than one-third of the respondents had their students visit a school library or invited a teacher-librarian to the class. While attempts such as these to integrate information about

TABLE 2. Methods Used by Teacher Educators to Inform Pre-Service Teachers About the School Library

Method	Frequency
None	13
Guest speaker	10
Class discussion	10
Visit to school library	8
Work with teacher-librarian	7
Pamphlet	5
Lecture	1
Video	0

Note: Some respondents used more than one method.

school libraries into course content are useful, the overall impact of such efforts is greatly limited by the fact that fully one-half of respondents said they do nothing to include the role of the school library in their methods courses.

Information from the interviews also indicated that explicit teaching of the role of a school library in teacher education programs is rare. Classroom discussions do arise about where pre-service teachers will find resources or as a response to a recent practicum experience where returning students complain that they had to do the teacher-librarian's job in the school and yet they were not being prepared by the faculty to do this. On the other hand, the notion of a "self-fulfilling prophecy" was also raised several times. Course instructors reported that, even when "we do mention the school library," pre-service teachers report that there are no school libraries in their school or no staff person who can help them. On the one hand, then, nothing is being done to include information about school libraries or visits to working teacher-librarians in the pre-service education offered in provinces or districts where there are active school library programs. On the other hand, ironically, where some small efforts are being made to include the school library as an important part of teaching, pre-service teachers get out into the system and find there are not teacher-librarians working to support them.

Finally, several interviewees commented on today's generation of pre-service teachers who "have a strong belief we can do it alone. There is no need for the mediating role of the teacher-librarian. They don't see the need for the role and they don't understand how it works." This does not bode well for any attempt to revitalize the attention given to the role of the school library in future pre-service programs.

Preparation of Pre-Service Teachers for Information Literacy Instruction

A review of the literacy and social studies methods course objectives showed that information literacy skills are partially included:

- to teach students to assess the value of Internet resources, like a relevant Web site;
- to identify the importance of critical, visual, information, and media literacies in the language arts curriculum;
- to make use of resources such as the Internet in the development of lessons based on different types of literacy; and
- to collect a wide range of resource materials and evaluate these sources for use in the classroom.

These objectives indicate a fragmented and limited information literacy curriculum in which students develop these learning outcomes for their course work rather than for their future teaching. In other words, pre-service teachers learn information skills out of necessity to support their own learning, but the pedagogical applications of information literacy are not fully addressed in their coursework. Other insights into the inclusion of information literacy instruction in pre-service education programs were gained by asking instructors and library staff about the place of resource-based learning and research skills/strategies in methods courses and Education Library programs and services. There were 21 affirmative responses to the inclusion of these areas in the program and 11 negative responses. Thus, pre-service teachers are likely to learn about resource-based learning and how to plan and teach research units and the skills and strategies required to carry them out.

Research or information skills, when they are taught to pre-service teachers, are formulated as part of "content literacy" or skills necessary for learning from textbooks and informational texts. Students are expected to develop lesson plans focussed on these skills for use in their research units. Library staff claim that they provide knowledge and tools to pre-service teachers to facilitate their ability to teach information literacy. However, it appears that transfer of learned skills in the library to classroom instruction is not scaffolded enough for new teachers to be successful. Instead, faculty and library staff hope that "through students' own learning experiences in the courses, they will be able to apply their newly acquired skills in the classroom."

Instructors themselves model resource-based learning in their courses and students prepare files of resources for use in their teaching. However, only one instructor mentioned teaching students specific selection criteria (readability and student interest) for their resource files, and only one instructor noted any focus on Web resource evaluation.

As the interviewees discussed the inclusion of information literacy instruction in the pre-service programs, their responses ranged from "I assume all my students know everything about conducting research," to examples of course assignments in which related provincial learning outcomes are emphasized. The problem with these assignments is that most of the examples to which pre-service teachers may be exposed are learning outcomes associated with a particular subject area like language arts and social studies. Students are not taught that many of these outcomes are actually information literacy outcomes and that they apply across curricular areas. It seems "they are doing it and don't know it as information literacy." In addition, interdisciplinary approaches were non-existent in the programs we explored.

Many information literacy outcomes are addressed in courses dealing with the use of information technology. However, it was evident that "information technology people have taken on the role of information literacy specialists, but they are only focussed on Internet sites and finding the best ones for curriculum uses. They need to be shown that they need to teach critical literacy no matter what resources you are accessing."

The library staff interviewed seemed frustrated trying to get more professors "involved with the library." Many of the professors "see this work as important but they don't follow through. If Faculty members are not doing it within their own courses, then the pre-service teachers are not getting it."

The major consensus that emerged from the interviews was the awareness that "information literacy is changing everything." No longer are pre-service teachers sent to find resources or to gather resources in a folder; now "what they have to do is sort out what is useful and reliable and appropriate and so information literacy is more important than ever." However, if "it is not going to be the school library that models and leads these things, then we have to teach all pre-service teachers how to do it. It is embedded in all curriculum, so someone has to teach it."

CONCLUSIONS AND DIRECTIONS

Data analysis showed that school libraries are not playing much of a role in the preparation of pre-service teachers in the 17 Faculty of Education programs we examined. It was disheartening at best, and a serious call for action for the library community across the country. Our findings can be summarized in this way:

1. There is clear evidence of a serious neglect of school library education in the 17 Faculties of Education we examined. In most cases, participants reported that "the topic never comes up" and that "everyone assumes someone else is dealing with the matter."
2. We identified weak or no alternative practices for introducing pre-service teachers to the role of the school library in their future teaching career. Pre-service teachers receive only cursory refer-

ence to the role of a school library and little or no practicum experience with school libraries when they get to the schools.

3. Information literacy pedagogy is not explicitly developed in these 17 pre-service programs and there appears to be no expectations that pre-service teachers transfer the learning experiences in methods courses to their actual classroom practice. It is assumed that by completing assignments with a strong connection to information literacy learning outcomes, the pre-service teachers will develop similar outcomes with their future students.

4. Respondents to the questionnaires and the interviews repeated over and over that they had not considered the school library in any explicit way in their work with pre-service teachers and their participation in the study served as "a wake-up call." They unanimously requested copies of the results of this study to share with their Faculty of Education colleagues and they suggested we develop information packages and teaching strategies that could be included in the Faculty's program.

5. The Staff working the education libraries in these Faculties of Education clearly understood the concept of information literacy and its pervasive role in their daily work with students and faculty members. They could identify many areas where the need for information literacy was essential in the teacher education program and they were excited by some of the collaborative program ideas we shared during the interviews. The librarians were actively seeking ways to connect their library programs with pre-service teachers' learning and course instructional goals. In the words of one education librarian, "we need to stop acting like academic libraries and start acting like school libraries."

While we gained significant information about the three research topics, what was most revealing was the exposure of our naivety of other teacher educators' understandings of the role of the school library in education. It became clear we were speaking a different language from those involved in teacher education, and by implication, from those in schools. As well, we were surprised by the extent that Faculties of Education have forgotten the role of the teacher-librarian and the value of school libraries in our educational system. Either much of what school libraries purport to contribute to education is already being done in other ways or we had better start targeting teacher education programs as part of a national strategy to raise awareness and offer support to Faculties of Education trying to revitalize this all but forgotten part of education. Given the value of attaining information literacy standards within the context of inquiry-based learning, integrated approaches to learning, and embedded use of information technology in modern educational policy and curriculum, the time is ripe for ensuring new teachers are informed about the leadership role school libraries play in these areas. There is little evidence that information literacy is given high priority in Canadian schools, despite known requirements of the knowledge-based economy and the inclusion of information literacy in desired characteristics of Canadian employees (Whitehead & Quinlan, 2002, p. 8). This trend will continue if new teachers remain unequipped to teach information literacy through collaboration in effective school library programs.

The school library community needs to reposition its role in light of significant developments in wider educational reform and in teacher education programs and start to include new teachers in professional development activities. Teacher-librarians need to seek out opportunities to have a pre-service teacher do a practicum in the school library. They need to meet with all pre-service teachers when they start their practicum and show them how school libraries can advance student achievement and add creative energy to their classroom programs. Teacher librarian organizations need to collaborate with teacher educators to provide pre-service teachers with authentic information literacy lesson planning experiences as part of their required coursework (Asselin & Lee, 2002). Our colleagues working in Faculty of Education Resource Libraries hold out great hope for the modelling of the role of the teacher-librarian in Faculty of Education programs. We need to share some of the fine examples of how a qualified librarian working in an academic library can collaborate with Faculty members and students to integrate resources and create exciting learning experiences.

While the challenges are great, our study has begun to point the Canadian school library field towards effective ways of reinventing teacher preparation. We have also identified models that correct teacher education programs where "pre-service teachers do not often experience authentic assessment, collaborative teaching, the use of technology in integrated settings, or learning through an integrated curriculum" (Stokes, Kaufman, & Lacey, 2002/2003). We certainly don't want the words of Bliss Carmen's poem, *The Vagabond*, to be the final epitaph of school libraries in Canada, "they come and go without our knowing whence they come and whither they go."

REFERENCES

Asselin, Marlene, and Elizabeth Lee. 2002. "I wish someone had taught me": Information literacy in a teacher education program. *Teacher Librarian* 30 (2): 10-17.

American Association of School Librarians and the Association for Educational Communications and Technology. 1998. *Information power: Building partnerships for learning.* Chicago: American Library Association.

Association for Teacher-librarianship in Canada and the Canadian School Library Association. 1997. *Students' information literacy needs: Competencies for teacher-librarians in the 21st century* [online]. Ottawa, Ontario: Canadian Library Association [cited 31 January 2003]. Available from World Wide Web: <http://www.cla.ca/divisions/csla/pub_2.htm>.

Carr, Jo Ann. 1998. *Information literacy and teacher education* [online]. Washington, DC: ERIC Clearinghouse on Teaching and Teacher Education. (ERIC Document Reproduction Service No. ED424231) [cited 25 January 2003]. Available from World Wide Web: <http://www.ericfacility.net/ericdigests/ed424231.html>.

Council of Ministers of Education, Canada (1999). *Shared priorities in education at the dawn of the 21st century: Future directions for The Council of Ministers of Education, Canada* [online]. Toronto, Ontario: The Author [cited 27 January 2003]. Available from World Wide Web: <http://www.cmec.ca/reports/victoria99.en.stm>.

Hargreaves, Andy. 1995. *Changing teachers, changing times: Teachers' work and culture in the postmodern age.* New York: Teachers College Press.

International Society for Technology Education. 2000-2002. *National educational technology standards* [online]. Eugene, OR: The Author [cited 28 January 2003]. Available from World Wide Web: <http://cnets.iste.org/>.

Media Awareness Network. (2002). *Welcome to the Media Awareness Network* [online]. Ottawa, Ontario: The Author [cited 27 January 2003]. Available from World Wide Web: <http://www.media-awareness.ca/eng/>.

National Commission on Teaching and America's Future. 1996. *What matters most: Teaching for America's future: Report of the National Commission on Teaching and America's Future* [online]. New York: The Author [cited 27 January 2003]. Available from World Wide Web: <http://www.nctaf.org/publications/WhatMattersMost.pdf>.

National Council of Teachers of English and the International Reading Association. 1996. *Standards for the English language arts* [online]. Urbana, IL: National Council of Teachers of English [cited 19 December 2002]. Available from World Wide Web: <http://www.ncte.org/standards/standards.shtml>.

Shapson, S. M. 1998. Teacher education at a turning point. *Orbit* 29 (2): 10-14.

Stokes, Sandra M., Timothy U. Kaufman, and Arthur Lacey. 2002. Preparing teachers of the 21st century: Creating technological literacy in a teacher education program. *Reading Online* 6 (5) [online] [cited 27 January 2003]. Available from World Wide Web: <http://www.readingonline.org/articles/art_index.asp?HREF=stokes/index.html>.

Western and Northern Canadian Protocol. 2003. Western Canadian protocol for collaboration in education: Common curriculum framework [online]. N.P.: The Author [cited 26 January 2003]. Available World Wide Web: <http://www.wcp.ca/>.

Whitehead, Martha J., and Quinlan, Catherine A. 2002. *Canada: An information literacy case study*. White paper prepared for UNESCO, the U.S. National Commission on Libraries, Information Sciences, and the National Forum on Information Literacy [online]. Washington, DC: National Commission on Libraries and Information Science [cited 26 January 2003]. Available World Wide Web: <http://www.nclis.gov/libinter/infolitconf&meet/papers/quinlan-fullpaper.pdf>.

Teaching, Learning and Information Literacy: Developing an Understanding of Pre-Service Teachers' Knowledge

Jennifer L. Branch

SUMMARY. This study explored pre-service teachers' understandings of information literacy and Information and Communication Technology (ICT) outcomes before and after being involved in a class that promoted and explored issues of information literacy and resource-based learning. One surprising result of a pre-class questionnaire was that, when asked about the role of information literacy in their lives as teachers, only four of the ten participants mentioned the students in their classroom and only one participant clearly stated that information literacy skills would need to be taught to students. This result suggests that teacher educators need to move from helping pre-service teachers become more information literate to helping pre-service teachers integrate information literacy skills into their own teaching. The post-class questionnaire found that immersing pre-service teachers in a research process, information literacy, and re-

Jennifer L. Branch is Coordinator, Teacher-Librarianship by Distance Learning Program and Assistant Professor with a joint appointment in the Department of Education and the School of Library and Information Studies, Faculty of Education, University of Alberta, Edmonton, AB, Canada (E-mail: jbranch@ualberta.ca).

[Haworth co-indexing entry note]: "Teaching, Learning and Information Literacy: Developing an Understanding of Pre-Service Teachers' Knowledge." Branch, Jennifer L. Co-published simultaneously in *Behavioral & Social Sciences Librarian* (The Haworth Information Press, an imprint of The Haworth Press, Inc.) Vol. 22, No. 1, 2003, pp. 33-46; and: *Information Literacy Instruction for Educators: Professional Knowledge for an Information Age* (ed: Dawn M. Shinew, and Scott Walter) The Haworth Information Press, an imprint of The Haworth Press, Inc., 2003, pp. 33-46. Single or multiple copies of this article are available for a fee from The Haworth Document Delivery Service [1-800-HAWORTH, 9:00 a.m. - 5:00 p.m. (EST). E-mail address: docdelivery@haworthpress.com].

Digital Object Identifier: 10.1300/J103v22n01_04

source-based learning environment allowed their definitions of information literacy to expand, and they were better able to imagine how they could integrate the ICT outcomes into their teaching. *[Article copies available for a fee from The Haworth Document Delivery Service: 1-800-HAWORTH. E-mail address: <docdelivery@haworthpress.com> Website: <http://www.Haworth Press.com> © 2003 by The Haworth Press, Inc. All rights reserved.]*

KEYWORDS. Information literacy, teacher education, resource-based learning, information and communication technology, research process

Information literacy is one of the educational buzzwords for this new millennium. As educators, we want our students to be able to locate, evaluate, synthesize, and use information from a variety of sources to answer all types of questions. As teacher educators, our challenge is to prepare teachers to teach the skills, strategies and attitudes that are part of information literacy. Education librarians can have an important role in the information literacy education of pre-service teachers as well.

The research in this paper was conducted in the Faculty of Education at the University of Alberta. Readers outside of Canada should be aware of the Canadian educational context. By legislation, education, including post-secondary education, is primarily a provincial and territorial matter. There have recently been a number of regional initiatives deigned to create common curriculum frameworks in the areas of math, language arts, science and social studies. As yet, there is neither a national office of education, nor national governmental policies in the areas of information literacy and technology integration for pre-service teachers or for K-12 students. Some regional, provincial and territorial policy initiatives in these areas have been developed, however, or are in the development stage, including Alberta's Information and Communication Technology Curriculum.

It is also important to know that there are two national school library associations, neither having the impact on educational policy and practice of the kind evidenced in the U.S. by organizations such as the American Association of School Librarians (AASL) and the International Society for Technology in Education (ISTE). Nor are teacher education institutions in Canada accredited by a body equivalent to the National Council for Accreditation of Teacher Education (NCATE). As is consistent with the Canadian approach to many aspects of public policy, assurance of high-quality programs and services does not come about through federal regulations but through more local and collaborative processes of negotiation underpinned by expectations of goodwill, effort and integrity.

It was in this educational climate that the province of Alberta and its education department (Alberta Learning) created the Information and Communication Technology (ICT) outcomes. Information literacy is part of this new document that "provides students with a broad perspective on the nature of technology, how to use and apply a variety of technologies, and the impact of information and communication technologies on themselves and on society" (Alberta Learning 2002). The ICT curriculum is meant to be integrated with other K-12 curriculum areas.

The ICT curriculum focuses on new ways to "communicate, inquire, make decisions and solve problems. It is the processes, tools and techniques for:

- Gathering and identifying information
- Classifying and organizing
- Summarizing and synthesizing
- Analyzing and evaluating
- Speculating and predicting" (Alberta Learning, 2002).

These concepts are presented in three categories. The first, "communicating, inquiring, decision making and problem solving are about the ability to use a variety of processes to critically assess information, manage inquiry, solve problems, do research and communicate with a variety of audiences. Students are expected to apply their knowledge and skills in real-life situations." The second category, foundational operations, knowledge and concepts, is "about understanding the nature and effect of technology, the moral and ethical use of technology, mass media in a digitized context, ergonomic and safety issues, and basic computer, telecommunication and multimedia technology operations." Processes for productivity, the third category, "is about the knowledge and skills required to use a variety of basic productivity tools and techniques–for example, text composition; data organization; graphical, audio and multimedia composition and manipulation; media and process integration; and electronic communication, navigation and collaboration through electronic means" (Alberta Learning 2002).

These outcomes are not that different from expectations across North America that teachers integrate technology and information literacy skills into teaching. In Alberta, as in other jurisdictions, school districts have implemented professional development and in-service sessions for their classroom teachers in order to facilitate this work. In Faculties of Education, some methods courses now include reference to, and assignments based on, the ICT outcomes. Also, students have been required to take a computer fundamentals class that focuses on the technology outcomes from ICT. At the University of Alberta, information literacy is not specifically addressed.

We know very little about what understandings pre-service teachers have about information literacy and how a course that promotes information literacy influences these understandings. This study explored pre-service teachers' understandings of information literacy and ICT outcomes. Pre-service teachers were involved in a class on resource-based teaching that promoted and explored issues of information literacy and resource-based learning. Early in the class, participants were asked about their understandings of information literacy. At the end of the class, they were again asked about their understandings of information literacy and also about ICT outcomes to compare and contrast with the initial responses.

REVIEW OF THE LITERATURE

As early as 1989, the American Library Association recommended that information literacy be included in pre-service teacher education. In 1998, when the Association of College and Research Libraries (ACRL) prepared *A Progress Report on Information Literacy: An Update on the American Library Association Presidential Committee on Information Literacy: Final Report,* they were able to "outline the astounding progress that has been made toward the reaching of these recommendations in such a relatively short period of time, with little financial support, and largely through volunteer and grassroots efforts." However, one glaring area where nothing had been accomplished was Recommendation 5–teacher education and information literacy. ACRL (1998) suggested that there must be a "plan for working with teacher education programs and the National Council for Accreditation of Teacher Education to infuse information literacy requirements into undergraduate and graduate programs of teacher education." The call for information literacy to be included in pre-service teacher education was made again in *Blueprint for Collaboration* (ACRL 2000) with the statement that faculties of education need to "include academic librarians as members of the instructional team in graduate and undergraduate teacher education programs and in continuing professional teacher development programs."

Elsewhere in this collection, Asselin and Doiron (2003) report on a study of the role of school libraries and information literacy in Faculties of Education at universities across Canada. They discovered that activities that foster information literacy skills were included in the course content of methods courses in pre-service education. However, these information literacy outcomes were aimed at facilitating the pre-service teachers' own school success rather than toward helping pre-service teachers think about how they would teach information literacy skills in their own classrooms. According to the authors, "The skills associated with information literacy such as working with the research process are very much a part of revitalized methods courses, but little is done to show pre-service teachers how to develop these skills with their future students." In fact, "it appears that transfer of learned skills in the library to classroom instruction is not scaffolded enough for new teachers to be successful." In speaking with librarians at libraries and resource centers that serve the Faculties of Education, the authors found that librarians were also helping pre-service teachers develop information literacy skills–even if the librarians did not always recognize that they were doing so. Disheartening to hear was that librarians reported that they were not aware of leadership in the area of information literacy by any of the course instructors.

Asselin and Lee (2002) reported the results of a study where they infused information literacy into a language arts methods course for pre-service teachers. The authors used pre- and post-reflective writings and concept maps or webs as a way to track the new understandings of information literacy. They found that students' information literacy knowledge was enhanced by participating in the project. For Asselin and Lee (2002), "the most significant development in our students' understanding of information literacy was the shift from thinking of it as 'reading masses of print information' to 'a process-based view of interpreting and generating multiple types of information'" (13). Participants were very excited about how their information literacy skills improved during the course. They felt, for example, that they were better able to use and to teach students how to use electronic resources and to search the Internet.

RESEARCH METHODS

This study focused on information literacy understandings and the effects of an information-literacy class on a group of pre-service teacher education students. The University of Alberta offers two Bachelor of

Education programs–a four-year program and two-year program for those students who already have a degree. The participants in the study were enrolled in Resource-Based Teaching (EDES 346), a course offered to students in both the elementary and secondary streams. The class had 20 students (17 women and 3 men) ranging in age from about 20 to 45.

The course involved exploring a variety of resources (e.g., encyclopedias and other reference tools, the ERIC database, Web sites, books, online and print newspapers and magazines, scholarly journal articles, games, videos, and posters) and creating an annotated bibliography on a topic from the curriculum of the student's choice. Students were also required to prepare a critical evaluation of a Web site, to create a poster presentation on a community resource to support teaching and learning, and to plan an integrated resource-based teaching unit that incorporated one or more content areas plus ICT outcomes. These assignments were designed to allow pre-service teachers to learn about research while completing a research process leading up to the production of the integrated, resource-based teaching unit. Pre-service teachers chose a topic of interest from a preferred curriculum area (usually the student's major or minor) and created an annotated bibliography of resources useful to support teaching and learning for their topic. Next, pre-service teachers evaluated a Web site that would be useful for their topic and, finally, identified community resources that would support their topic. Using all of these resources, pre-service teachers then developed their unit. The course focused on helping pre-service teachers understand how to locate, evaluate, and use appropriate teaching and learning resources in a variety of formats to develop an integrated resource-based learning unit. It also highlighted research process models, learning styles, authentic assessment, school library programs (including visits to school libraries at the elementary, junior and senior high level), inquiry-based learning, planning a resource-based learning project, and how to promote reading in schools.

An education librarian assisted with the class by doing two workshops. The first workshop was an orientation to the library and to the resources that would be especially important for the students including reference materials and the reference librarians' information desk, current journals, newspapers and magazines, curriculum documents, and the curriculum library. The curriculum library is located within the education library and collects all of the selected and approved resources for Alberta schools. The second workshop was an ERIC database-searching workshop. Education librarians have a long history collaborating with instructors and faculty members in developing and teaching this class.

Research ethics approval was given by the Faculty of Education to carry out the study. Participants gave informed consent and were not coerced in any way. The researcher was also the instructor so it was important for the students to understand that the decision to participate or not had no influence on grades. All students in the class were asked to participate and ten volunteered. The ten participants represent students of varying ages and home life situations.

The pre-service teachers came with a variety of backgrounds and more than half of the participants had already completed a degree in another subject area such as biology, mathematics, accounting, chemistry, or English. Six of the ten participants had taken a course in computer fundamentals that highlighted some of the ICT outcomes (those relating to specific technologies, e.g., spreadsheets, databases, word-processing programs, Web design, presentation software, and digital imaging software). Additional opportunities exist for pre-service teachers to attend workshops in the Education Library but these are all on a voluntary basis. Students may be exposed to information literacy discussions as part of other courses but not in any structured way. A newly-designed required course in educational technology now involves information literacy instruction by education librarians, but these participants were not involved in that course.

Each of the participants completed two open-ended questionnaires that were distributed on the course Web site and returned by e-mail. The first questionnaire asked about the participant's family life, work life and school life, about the participant's understanding of the term information literacy, and about the participant's understanding of how information literacy will be a part of his or her professional life as a teacher. The second questionnaire asked questions about the impact of the course including changes to the participant's understanding of the term information literacy, how information literacy will be a part of his or her own teaching, and if the participant felt more information literate as a result of the class. Questions also were asked about the participant's understandings of the ICT outcomes mandated for all schools in Alberta. The first questionnaire was distributed early in the term (September 2002), and the second at the end of the term (December 2002).

Each of the questionnaires arrived by e-mail so no transcription of responses was necessary. Each set of responses was read thoroughly. As the research progressed, e-mail responses and observation notes were analyzed to generate ideas, thoughts and new questions. Patterns and common experiences emerged from the data and were recorded.

Participants also gave the researcher permission to analyze the final examination that asked them to "describe the purpose of the Information and Communication Technology Outcomes and how you would integrate those outcomes into your own teaching." This data also provided insight into the students' understanding of information literacy and how to integrate these skills into the curriculum.

FINDINGS

Several themes emerged from the data analysis. These include Definitions of Information Literacy, Information Literacy in Teaching and Learning, Becoming Information Literate, and the Impact of the Course on Understanding and Being Able to Integrate ICT Outcomes. Each of these themes is presented below.

Definitions of Information Literacy

Participants were all able to define information literacy. Information literacy for the majority of the participants had to do with "finding," "locating," and "acquiring" information in various forms. For four participants, it also meant being able to "use" the information. One participant stated, "I think it means many things–being able to understand a question being posed to you, being able to communicate with others, knowing where to look for pertinent information, being able to sort through all of the gobbledygook to find what it is you were looking for, knowing the difference between different sources." The idea of being able to tell the "difference between credible and less credible sources" came up only one other time. Three participants also talked about the need to understand information that comes from different kinds of sources.

There were some similarities and differences from the first questionnaire, when participants were asked about their information literacy understandings, and their responses to the same question at the end of the term. Participants still strongly indicated that "finding," "locating," and "accessing" information were very important in information literacy. New terms, however, entered the definitions, including "process," "brainstorm," "organize," "calculate," and "solve." Several of the participants, when asked if their definition of information literacy had changed answered in the negative, and then proceeded to give a completely different definition from the one offered earlier. One of the participants noted that she felt that being information literate was "more important" than she had before the course: "I think that it [information literacy] has, however, grown in importance for me. I think it is becoming even more important for people to be able to understand and evaluate the validity of the information that they receive in every day life, especially with the growing influence of the media." Another student noted that "Now I include the ability to calculate and solve mathematical problems as a function of information literacy."

Information Literacy in Teaching and Learning

Participants also had many ideas about the ways information literacy will be a part of their lives as teachers. One noted that she "will need to be able to find information to supplement information given in the textbook." Along the same lines, another stated that she "will always be looking for updated information as well as focusing on the best method to teach a particular subject." A third added: "Teachers get sent all sorts of stuff, and have to balance all sorts of outside interests in their classroom so being able to sort through all the information that's available (from all sorts of sources, and whether I want the info or not!), and pick out the stuff/resources that I need and that will be useful to me would be helpful." There was certainly a strong message that participants felt that they needed to be information literate to help themselves as teachers.

Only four of the ten participants gave some indication that it was important to help their students become information literate. Only one got to the heart of the issue of teaching information literacy. She stated, "I would also like to think that I'll be passing skills other than the primary subject to my students as well–things such as how to organize, how to wade through information to find what's really important, etc." One participant wanted her students to be information literate and another wanted students to be independent learners. A third participant noted that it was "important to be able to teach students how to find information, especially now when there is so much information out there. I cannot possibly teach them everything so they need to know how to find out information on their own."

Becoming Information Literate

When asked if participants felt more information literate as a result of this class, all felt that they were. Some of the things participants felt they had learned included:

- the ability to identify an information need and to think critically about the best resources available to meet that need;
- the ability to access community resources to locate information;
- the ability to critically evaluate information found on the Internet; and,
- the ability to present students with different styles of projects.

One student stated, "I think that I am more information literate. I am better able to access computer-based information, am aware of ways to evaluate information and feel that I am able to take the information I have learned and use it in my classroom." Participants did suggest areas where they still felt unsure about information literacy. These included the more practical things such as searching the Internet and understanding the different search engines, searching online databases including ERIC, and learning how to use the library.

Impact of Course on Understanding and Being Able to Integrate ICT Outcomes

The ICT outcomes are the closest thing to an information literacy curriculum that one could hope to have–nearly 20 percent of the committee developing the curriculum was made up of teacher-librarians. When asked about understandings about ICT outcomes, seven of the ten participants felt they were better able to address ICT outcomes as a result of this class. One stated, "I never realized they weren't all about computers–all of my curriculum classes emphasized the use of computers, but not the thinking and learning that comes with the technology and piles of information." Another commented, "I know where to find them now! Now that I know where they are, then I can better address them through different activities." A third added, "Yes, I do feel better able to address ICT outcomes, if only because I was forced to look at them and see how they would apply to my classroom and I hadn't been asked to do that before." Other students felt that previous courses had also prepared them in this regard. One noted that the required computer course and her minor course "did a good job of addressing ICT outcomes." Another felt that the required computer course was more useful to her for addressing ICT outcomes. As she wrote: "I feel better knowing about ICT outcomes but not to fully address all the issues."

Participants had many ideas for integrating ICT outcomes into the curriculum and these included having students:

- Retrieve, access, and critically evaluate information from a variety of sources;
- Use and learn more advanced skills on available software such as Inspiration, PowerPoint, FrontPage, Excel, and Word;
- Learn to use, manipulate, and incorporate digital images, digital videos, graphics, clip art and drawings to enhance presentations;
- Learn to properly cite sources;
- Research a variety of authentic topics with real world applications and using real world data to learn different points of view; and,
- Incorporate graphics, clip art, and drawings.

DISCUSSION

Early in the resource-based teaching course, the ten participants were able to give a very limited definition of information literacy. Their definitions included finding/locating/accessing information, and some included using/evaluating/selecting information. Although the definitions were not complete and did not include the idea of process, this was not unexpected. What was surprising, however, was that when asked about the role of information literacy in their life as a teacher only four of the ten participants mentioned the students in their classroom and only one clearly stated that information literacy skills would need to be taught to students. When examining the results of research done by Asselin and Doiron (in press), however, it became clear why this was happening. Pre-service teachers are indeed being taught information literacy skills as part of their methods courses, but these methods courses are not helping pre-service teachers prepare to integrate and teach information literacy skills to the students in their own classrooms.

The failure to connect information literacy skills to teachers' future students is the fatal flaw in our current pre-service education programs. Either as teacher educators or as education librarians, we need to move from simply helping pre-service teachers become more information literate themselves to preparing pre-service teachers to integrate information literacy skills into their own teaching (which should also help pre-service teachers become more information literate). Asselin and Lee (2002) found success with integrating information literacy instruction into a language arts methods course for pre-service teachers. They found the project made "a difference to new teachers' understanding of and abilities to teach information literacy" (16).

This study confirmed the findings of Asselin and Lee (2002) and found that by immersing pre-service teachers in a research process, information literacy, and resource-based learning environment, their definitions of information literacy expanded and they were better able to imagine how they could integrate the ICT outcomes into their teaching. Moreover, they felt more comfortable with integrating the ICT outcomes into their lessons and the variety of ways they envisioned doing so is proof of this.

IMPLICATIONS AND CONCLUSIONS

We all wish for our children to grow up to be independent, life-long learners. Consequently, our children will need the information literacy skills of being able to identify, locate, and effectively use information to solve all kinds of problems. For Carr (1998), "this ability to learn how to learn is a key characteristic of those who are information literate." These skills need to be taught to our children, beginning at an early age, and need to be reinforced and expanded as they move through elementary, junior and senior high school. A few parents may be able to help their children learn these skills but classroom teachers and teacher-librarians will have the most responsibility for developing these skills.

For that to happen we must ensure that our pre-service teachers learn in their teacher education programs the skills not only to be information literate teachers, but also to be information literacy instructors. This process may actually involve two steps. The first is to develop the information literacy skills in our pre-service teachers. We look to education librarians, teacher educators, and other instructors in undergraduate programs to work with post-secondary students to require them to find, evaluate, use, synthesize, and present information in interesting ways using a variety of technologies. The second step is that Faculties of Education must recognize that having information literate teachers does not necessarily mean that they will produce information literate students. We do not expect that people who are good in science and math will inherently understand the strategies and methods appropriate for teaching others to be good in science and math. Likewise, we cannot assume that the fact that one has mastered the research process means that one is prepared to effectively integrate information skills instruction as part of the coursework in a content area. In teacher education programs we help pre-service teachers understand both the content and the strategies necessary to teach a particular subject such as language arts, social studies, math and science. Effective teachers need to have the content and understandings of information literacy and also the discussion of strategies, methods, and approaches that best suit the teaching of information literacy, including the importance of integrating information literacy skills instruction into all subject areas.

Teacher educators must rethink and redesign methods courses. Along with helping pre-service teachers develop their own information literacy skills, we also need to make it a priority for them to understand how to teach information literacy to their students. In this way, we can help pre-service teachers to become lifelong learners who can then promote lifelong learning skills in their own classrooms. For that to happen, pre-service teachers need to be given opportunities to see how information literacy skills can be integrated into the core subject areas and how important new technologies can be when finding, organizing, synthesizing and presenting information.

Perhaps we can do this easily within existing methods courses by rethinking assignments (Asselin and Lee 2002), or maybe we must create a new course, required for all pre-service teachers, that provides opportunities to learn how to integrate information literacy instruction into their lessons while exploring issues of process learning, information technology and resource-based learning. Either way, we need to find new ways to help pre-service teachers gain these skills.

To effect change, we need reports of other projects designed to help pre-service teachers become more information literate. Examples such as these, including those provided in this collection, can provide teacher education program planning committees with models of possibilities and options for course revisions and additions. We also need more research to help us to better understand how to support and guide pre-service teachers when they are learning to be information literacy teachers. These pre-service teachers can be the ones who can help our children meet the challenges of living in the Information Age.

REFERENCES

Alberta Learning. 2002. *Information communication and technology* [online]. [cited 11 September 2002]. Available from World Wide Web: <http://www.learning.gov.ab.ca/k_12/curriculum/bySubject/ict/>.

American Library Association. 1989. *Final Report of the Presidential Committee on Information Literacy* [online]. Chicago: The Author [cited 10 March 2003]. Available from World Wide Web: <http://www.ala.org/acrl/nili/ilit1st.html>.

Asselin, Marlene, and Elizabeth A. Lee. 2002. "I wish someone had taught me": Information literacy in a teacher education program. *Teacher Librarian 30* (2): 10-17.

Asselin, Marlene, and Ray Doiron. 2003. Whither they go: An analysis of the inclusion of school library programs and services in the preparation of pre-service teachers in Canadian universities. *Behavioral and Social Sciences Librarian*, 22(1): 19-32.

Association of College and Research Libraries. 1998. *A progress report on information literacy: An update on the American Library Association Presidential Committee on Information Literacy: Final Report.* [cited 18 December 2002]. Available from World Wide Web: <http://www.ala.org/acrl/nili/nili.html>.

Association of College and Research Libraries and American Association of School Librarians. 2000. *Blueprint for Collaboration: AASL/ACRL Task Force on the Educational Role of Libraries.* [cited 88 January 20032]. Available from World Wide Web: <http://www.ala.org/acrl/blueprint.html>.

Carr, Jo Ann. 1998. *Information literacy and teacher education* [online]. Washington, DC: ERIC Clearinghouse on Teaching and Teacher Education. (ERIC Document Reproduction Service No. ED 424231) [cited 5 March 2003]. Available World Wide Web: <http://www.ericfacility.net/ericdigests/ed424231.html>.

A Flying Start for Our Future Teachers:
A Comprehensive
Information Literacy Program
for Pre-Service Education Students
at the University of Wollongong,
Australia

Suzanne Lipu

SUMMARY. The Education Faculty Librarian at the University of Wollongong has collaborated with the faculty's academic staff to develop a program to ensure that there is a planned, comprehensive approach to information literacy development for pre-service Education students. The program aims to provide students with the knowledge and skills to excel in their studies, their teaching, and their lifelong learning pursuits. Specific subjects have been targeted for information literacy to be significantly integrated into the academic curriculum. This article provides a detailed overview of the program as well as some background into its conception and development. It concludes with a reflection of the program after its first two years in practice and considers possible future directions. *[Article copies available for a fee from The Haworth Document Delivery Service: 1-800-HAWORTH. E-mail address: <docdelivery@haworthpress.com> Website: <http://www.HaworthPress.com> © 2003 by The Haworth Press, Inc. All rights reserved.]*

Suzanne Lipu is Education Faculty Librarian, University of Wollongong, Wollongong NSW 2522, Australia (E-mail: suzanne_lipu@uow.edu.au).

[Haworth co-indexing entry note]: "A Flying Start for Our Teachers: A Comprehensive Information Literacy Program for Pre-Service Education Students at the University of Wollongong, Australia." Lipu, Suzanne. Co-published simultaneously in *Behavioral & Social Sciences Librarian* (The Haworth Information Press, an imprint of The Haworth Press, Inc.) Vol. 22, No. 1, 2003, pp. 47-73; and: *Information Literacy Instruction for Educators: Professional Knowledge for an Information Age* (ed: Dawn M. Shinew, and Scott Walter) The Haworth Information Press, an imprint of The Haworth Press, Inc., 2003, pp. 47-73. Single or multiple copies of this article are available for a fee from The Haworth Document Delivery Service [1-800-HAWORTH, 9:00 a.m. - 5:00 p.m. (EST). E-mail address: docdelivery@haworthpress.com].

KEYWORDS. Information literacy, teacher education, collaboration with faculty, Australia

AN INTRODUCTION
TO AUSTRALIAN EDUCATIONAL TERMS

Throughout this paper there are a number of educational terms used that may differ from those used internationally. The following explanations may help to prevent confusion.

A *faculty* refers to a group of similar subject or discipline departments or schools. At the University of Wollongong there are nine faculties including Arts, Creative Arts, Commerce, Education, Engineering, Health and Behavioural Sciences, Informatics, Law and Science.

A *faculty librarian* is a subject specialist librarian or liaison librarian assigned to a specific academic faculty.

A *subject* refers to an individual unit of study (usually one semester in length) that is worth a certain number of credit points. A series of subjects make up a *course*–such as a Bachelor of Teaching (Primary Education) degree.

Tertiary literacies refer to the skill sets graduates are required to develop through their university studies. At the University of Wollongong the tertiary literacies include: academic literacy, information literacy, computer literacy, statistical literacy and professional literacy. It is intended that competence in these literacies help students achieve the attributes expected of a University of Wollongong graduate.

The *graduate attributes* drive teaching and learning at the university and refer to the qualities graduating students are expected to have attained through their studies at the university. The attributes of a Wollongong graduate include lifelong learning, information literacy, cultural awareness and others.

SETTING THE SCENE:
INFORMATION LITERACY
AT THE UNIVERSITY OF WOLLONGONG

The profile of information literacy in Australia, as in many other developed countries, continues to grow. In his keynote address at the Fourth National Information Literacy Conference, Todd (2000) recounted how the movement here gained momentum in the 1980s with the development of educational policy statements that endorsed "information skills" and how it was largely driven by librarians. He also stated that while any definition of information literacy is complex, much of the Australian literature on information literacy focuses on empowerment and on information literacy as the key to lifelong learning. This emphasis is particularly reflected in developments in the higher education sector in Australia.

Bundy (1999) and others have accurately noted that there are "few tertiary education institutions in Australia which do not now include in their mission statements reference to the fact that they aspire to prepare students for lifelong learning" (238). Most universities also have some statement about "graduate attributes" students are expected to gain from their experiences in these institutions and there is frequent reference to lifelong learning and/or information literacy. The Attributes of a Wollongong Graduate include: "A commitment to continued and independent learning, intellectual development, critical analysis and creativity" and "a basic understanding of information literacy and specific skills in acquiring, organizing and presenting information, particularly through computer-based activity." (These, and the other attributes, can be viewed at http://www.uow.edu.au/general/stratpln/guiding.html.)

At the same time, Bundy (1999) expressed what many educators within these institutions feel:

> The creation of a learning culture which produces graduates with a capacity and desire for lifelong learning in a rapidly changing, complex, and information over-abundant environment, requires a major shift in the educational paradigm and its resourcing. Many Australian universities are grappling with how that shift can be achieved at a time of great organisational change and reduced financial, human, library and other resources, due largely to a perplexingly narrow visioned federal government. (239)

This is just as accurate a statement today as it was five years ago, if not more so. Nevertheless there appears to be no shortage of committed librarians and other educators who continue to put enormous effort into the goal of fostering graduates who will have the capacity for lifelong learning and will therefore be enabled to make positive contributions to the society in which they live.

This commitment has been evident at the University of Wollongong for many years and the institution has long been recognized as one of the leaders in information literacy instruction in Australia. Since 1989

Library staff have played an integral role in the University's Working Parties on Comprehensive Literacies (now referred to as Tertiary Literacies). These parties were responsible for incorporating information literacy into University policy documentation and practice. Some of the ways this was achieved include:

- Recommending and gaining endorsement for an integrated model of information literacy with a compulsory element remaining outside the curricula (ILIP100);
- Allocating individual faculty librarians to each Faculty to enable increased information literacy instruction;
- Hosting information literacy forums to facilitate interaction and collaboration between academics and faculty librarians; and,
- Establishing professional development opportunities for faculty librarians responsible for information literacy instruction.

The University of Wollongong was one of the first universities in Australia to introduce a compulsory, zero-credit-point information literacy subject for all new undergraduates. This program, the Information Literacies Introductory Program (ILIP100), is one of the most significant information literacy initiatives at this University. Each semester new undergraduates participate in a face-to-face library class or undertake an equivalent online tutorial that introduces basic information literacy skills. These skills are aimed at helping students learn to use the Library's catalogue, interpret reading lists, understand the Library's Reserve collection, locate journals and other specific media such as videorecordings and gain basic understanding of plagiarism. Each student must submit an assignment via the Web based on the skills learned in the class and/or online. Students must achieve 100% in the assignment and have it completed by the end of their first semester of study. Failure to complete the program results in withdrawal of results. A compulsory, postgraduate student version of the ILIP100 program–to be called ILIP009–has recently been established and is being introduced Autumn session 2003. Both these programs ensure that all students have the opportunity to begin their information literacy development, and with the University's endorsement of these programs as compulsory subjects, there is the significant acknowledgement at this institution that information literacy is not solely a library issue.

Commitment and leadership in information literacy remains high on the University of Wollongong Library's agenda. In 1999 the Library introduced a highly successful program for academic staff entitled *Aca-*

demic Outreach. This program aimed to promote the use of the increasing amount of electronic resources available and to facilitate staff information literacy development. Using a comprehensive and systematic approach, faculty librarians conducted over 400 individual, tailored visits to academic staff at their desktops during 1999 and 2000. Among the many positive results of this program was a notable increase in the requests by academics for library classes for their students and the creation of a more proactive culture widening opportunities for further information literacy initiatives. A paper was presented about this program at the Australian Library and Information Association's Reference and Information Services Section's *Reveling in Reference* Symposium held in Melbourne in 2001 where there was much interest from participants who were eager to find out how to successfully establish a comprehensive, effective and efficient program that fostered information literacy among staff at their institutions (Lipu & Peisley 2001).

More recently the Library has established a new team with responsibility for facilitating the comprehensive application of the Australian Information Literacy Standards through the work undertaken by faculty librarians in conjunction with their faculties and other learning support units across the University. The Standards, adapted from the U.S. equivalent in 2000, have been endorsed by University Senate as part of the most recent version of the University's Tertiary Literacies Policy.

While these are certainly major information literacy achievements, there are many other smaller information literacy developments occurring–such as the program developed in collaboration with the Faculty of Education that is the focus of this paper–that are equally important in contributing to the information literacy goals of the University.

WORKING WITH THE FACULTY OF EDUCATION AT THE UNIVERSITY OF WOLLONGONG: THE FACULTY LIBRARIAN'S ROLE

The Faculty of Education at the University of Wollongong offers undergraduate and postgraduate coursework and research degrees. The main areas of study include: Early Childhood, Primary and Secondary Education, Physical Education and Health, Adult Education and Training, Educational Leadership, Language and Literacy, Information and Communications Technologies in Learning, Special Education and Teaching English to Speakers of Other Languages.

As mentioned earlier, the University of Wollongong allocated individual librarians to each of its faculties in 1990. As with other Australian universities, faculty librarians are generally non-academic staff who are based in their institution's libraries. At Wollongong the main responsibilities of faculty librarians revolve around providing information literacy education and training to students, staff, colleagues and the broader University community, providing information and research services, and collection development.

Every faculty librarian at Wollongong has membership on their individual Faculty's Education Committees (which report to the University's Education Committee under Academic Senate, the body responsible for University teaching and learning policy and practice). They also attend and participate in broader Faculty meetings and specialist Faculty committees as appropriate or as requested. Given the wide diversity in faculty cultures, there is variability in acceptance and participation of faculty librarians in Faculty events such as planning days. The Education Faculty at the University of Wollongong is one that has been very receptive in its inclusion of the current faculty librarian at many different forums and events and for providing opportunities for her involvement in such things as special grant projects since her appointment in 1999. Along with the University and Library management's support, the Faculty's culture and collegial relationship with the faculty librarian helped provide a suitable environment to lay some solid foundations for pre-service education students' information literacy development and give them a flying start to their future careers and lifelong learning pursuits.

THE PHILOSOPHY BEHIND THE COMPREHENSIVE INFORMATION LITERACY PROGRAM FOR PRE-SERVICE EDUCATION STUDENTS AT THE UNIVERSITY OF WOLLONGONG

Getting to know the Faculty's structure, culture and information literacy program/development is expected of new faculty librarians at the University of Wollongong. The first few months in the position was spent establishing rapport and developing relationships with academic staff, largely through the opportunity provided by the *Academic Outreach* program described above. Significant time was also dedicated to scanning and evaluating the information literacy activity that was already taking place, and to gathering information from the Reference Librarian who had been involved in much of the University's information literacy developments, from other faculty librarians and from literature searching and looking at other university library programs which were all part of the early phase development of this program. As a result of these activities several themes emerged which determined the need and possible benefits of having a comprehensive program in place. These themes revolved around haphazard instruction, evolving roles of pre-service Education students, curriculum integration and pedagogy of information literacy instruction.

First, there appeared to be a great deal of the "one-shot" library classes that MacDonald et al., speak of in describing an information literacy program at the University of Rhode Island. As with the situation they discovered, there had been many classes given to Education students at the University of Wollongong, including many demonstration-type sessions. While these classes reached large numbers of students, they were not part of a plan or strategy but depended "almost entirely on individual faculty members taking the initiative to request sessions in the library . . . Some students receive repetitive instruction while others receive only minimal instruction, or none at all" (MacDonald et al. 2000, 241). It seemed that one of the most effective ways to overcome this was to consider a more planned approach that would enable better consistency and, more importantly, real opportunities for information literacy development to occur over the period of a course, rather than hoping that students would pick up a "one-shot" class or two along the way and gain skills and knowledge from those in isolation of context or their own evolving roles at university throughout a course.

It is this latter point that was also considered to be a significant motivator to develop such a comprehensive program. Education students are perhaps unique in terms of developing information literacy competency. Through observation and discussion with staff and students it was apparent that there were clear evolving roles that our pre-service Education students seem to develop.

It seemed that much of the first year is spent learning to become a *university student* and becoming familiar with the nature of the teaching profession and with the terminology and theories related to the profession. Students seemed unfamiliar with many of the resources available in a university library or how and why to use them. They are also introduced to the practicum experience in this first year.

In the second year students seemed to be in a better position to start thinking of themselves as *future teachers*. They needed information skills and knowledge that was not just about getting their assignments done but focused on things like evaluating information appropriate to use with their classes. During much of the second year students were seen to focus on the University's Curriculum Resource Centre (where all the teaching resource material exists) rather than what they called the "big" library, i.e., the main library on campus where Education textbooks, literature and journals are kept.

The role of the pre-service students as *future teachers* obviously continued into the third and fourth years as they progressed along the course. They seemed to have greater awareness about their role in fostering information literacy development in their classrooms, or were at least in a better position to understand this than they were earlier on. It is this role that makes teaching education students, as opposed to students in other disciplines, unique in terms of information literacy development. They are not gaining the skills and knowledge solely for their own lifelong learning but have the opportunity and responsibility to do so for others. As Carr (1998) has said: "If teachers are to use information so that others can learn from them, then teachers must be information literate" (3). Others have suggested that teacher librarians alone should not have sole responsibility for information literacy instruction. Instead, the responsibility needs to shift more to teachers in schools (Langford 2002, 21).

Another significant evolving role of a pre-service education student was also apparent in the third and fourth years. In these years our Education students were expected to study more research-oriented subjects or topics that required more investigation (literature and otherwise). They needed more advanced skills and the knowledge to be able to do this, and it seemed as if there was a steep learning curve and a leap back to having to use the "big" library more and to re-learn things (such as searching electronic databases) that they had begun to use in the first year. Those who intended to pursue further degrees beyond the undergraduate courses also seemed to require more advanced instruction opportunities at this point. Hence, the third role seemed to be about becoming more *experienced students* with more advanced needs or what eventually became referred to in the program as *potential postgraduates.*

After observing the multiple roles taken on by pre-service education students as they progressed through the course of study, it seemed clear that their information literacy instruction needs could best be met through a comprehensive, programmatic approach.

The next very important factor that was considered in this phase of development was context. There has been a great deal of practice and research about information literacy taught within and outside the curriculum. Attitudes toward this more integrated approach have generally been favorable.

Patricia Senn Breivik and Gordon Gee (1989; cited in Grafstein 2002) "argue that the integration of the library into the college curriculum, a closing of the gap between the library and the classroom, is an essential component in developing information literate graduates" (2).

Australia's Christine Bruce, author of one of the world's first doctoral theses on information literacy entitled *Seven Faces of Information Literacy*, has said that "[information literacy], like phenomena such as teaching and learning, does not have a life of its own, rather it is a way of thinking and reasoning about aspects of subject matter" (Bruce 1997; cited in Bruce 2000, 210). She also says that "many dimensions of information literacy are closely related to the context" (Bruce 2000, 211).

In 1996 a Working Party on Comprehensive Information Literacies at the University of Wollongong was given a $20,000 grant, funded by the Strategic Development Fund for Teaching and Learning to investigate a curriculum-integrated approach to literacies. After extensive forums, site visits and other investigations, this Working Party recommended integration of information literacies as the preferred model with a compulsory element to remain outside the curricula (McGurk 1997). The compulsory element became ILIP100.

Other Australian universities have also favored the integrated approach. In developing an information literacy framework at the University of Queensland, Orr et al. (2001) said: "It has become clear that the 'one-off' demonstration-style information skills classes delivered out of curriculum context do not necessarily coincide with the students' need for information, are sometimes not valued by the students, and do not necessarily prepare them for the challenges of research, problem-solving and continuous learning" (457).

The Australian Information Literacy Standards include the statement: "Achieving information literacy fluency requires an understanding that such development is not extraneous to the curriculum but is woven into its content, structure, and sequence" (CAUL 2001, 3).

Regardless of the largely positive feelings toward integration, there has since been debate on terms like integration, context, etc. Bruce (2000) has said that "the very term 'curriculum integration' is a barrier to effective curriculum design as it suggests the need to 'add-on' yet more content or 'skills.'" She also refers to the principle of constructive alignment which "involves designing learning activities in such a way that students are required to change their usual ways of learning; for information literacy educators, this will usually mean designing learning strategies so that students learn through the process of effective information use." Finally, Bruce notes that this "would allow us to abandon the terminology such as 'curriculum integration' and replace it with phrases such as 'curriculum design for information literacy and lifelong learning'" (212).

The debate over integration and context is beyond the scope of this article. However, it should be noted that as the integrated model is the favored one at the University of Wollongong, it served as the underpinning for the development of the comprehensive information literacy program for our pre-service Education students.

The final significant factor in developing the program was about pedagogy. There is generally little argument that information literacy development is recursive and non linear. The Australian Information Literacy Standards state: "As students progress through their undergraduate years and graduate programs, they need to have repeated opportunities for seeking, evaluating, managing, and applying information gathered from multiple sources and obtained from discipline specific research methods" (CAUL 2001, 4). The U.S. Information Literacy Standards (upon which the first edition of the Australian standards are based) also make reference to this need.

In thinking about what the comprehensive program might look like, and keeping in mind all the factors mentioned here, it seemed apparent that there would also need to be opportunity for repetition throughout the course so that students could learn, reflect, evaluate, modify and continuously develop their skills and knowledge. There needed to be opportunities for demonstrated transferability of skills and knowledge so that the aim was to indeed develop an information literate person capable of problem-solving and employing lifelong learning habits.

PROGRAM DEVELOPMENT AND IMPLEMENTATION

It was unquestionable that if a program was to be developed and implemented successfully then collaboration with faculty staff was critical. How to best achieve this was given much thought and preparation. There has been a great deal of literature produced on this topic. Bundy (1999) claimed that most user education occurring in universities is largely reactive and suggested that academic librarians need to be more proactive and forceful. Chiste et al. (2000) use the analogy of utilizing army tactics in developing an information literacy program and say: "In the academic library, a successful strategy for infiltrating faculty lines and entrenching information literacy in the formal curriculum requires careful selection of personnel; rigorous intelligence gathering, to identify both allies and adversaries; and disciplined employment of both defensive and offensive tactics" (202).

Others say that there are many different approaches by different librarians. Westwood (in Chiste et al. 2000) says that individuals need to know their own strengths, styles, and philosophies in order to use "your own personal strategies to collaboration with your own teaching faculty" (203).

All of these points are valid and were put into practice in the development of this program. After spending the first few months of the position doing observation, analysis and evaluation of the Faculty's information literacy situation, a considered "plan of attack" began. It was a conscious and deliberate decision to use a top-down approach. While recognizing the absolute importance and significant impact that "grass-roots" staff would have on the program's success, it was determined that getting the key drivers in the Faculty on board and ready to lead the program to long-term success was essential. From the beginning, detailed record keeping of developments were kept for communication purposes in the Faculty and Library and for personal records.

First on the agenda was meeting individually with key people in the Faculty in early 2000. The first step was a series of meetings with the Acting Dean. She had played a leadership role in the University's Tertiary Literacies Working Party in 1998, helped develop the University's Information Literacy Policy and had begun mapping the Faculty's literacies against University documentation. Tapping into her strong interest and depth of knowledge about the literacies and the Faculty was undoubtedly a huge advantage in getting this program off the ground.

With the Acting Dean it was decided that the program would consist of three parts–one specific plan for each of the main programs of study for undergraduate students–Early Childhood, Primary, and Physical and Health Education. It was also decided that ILIP100–the compulsory Information Literacies Introductory Program for all new undergraduates–would form the basis for each of the plans. Furthermore, the initial program was to focus only on undergraduate students. Consideration for international and postgraduate students would be developed later and classes would largely continue to be based upon requests for these groups. Staff could still request classes for subjects that had not been targeted for integration.

There was mutual agreement that the program needed the involvement of as many staff as possible, and the Acting Dean was very frank about getting reluctant or non-committed staff on board. As Grafstein (2002) has said: "It has, in principle, become widely acknowledged that, if IL programs are to be successful, they cannot be deployed under the exclusive initiation, development, implementation, direction, and support of academic libraries along with the few committed and overworked classroom faculty whom librarians can convince to 'buy into' the enterprise by collaborating with them on select courses" (198). Had the Acting Dean not been so supportive, strategic, and proactive in her approach to supporting the development of this program, it may not have taken off so quickly or gained acceptance as readily.

With her endorsement and support the next step was to meet individually with each of the undergraduate course Directors. These meetings were used to:

- Establish rapport;
- Understand the content and structure of the different strands;
- Reach agreement that ILIP100 was the basis of each program; and,
- Identify and target one or two core and/or otherwise significant or "difficult" subjects for each year of study as the ones to be used for the information literacy integration.

The next step was to meet with each of the subject coordinators for the subjects chosen as targets. This was obviously more time-consuming and involved more than one meeting. The initial meeting was used to discuss the particular aims and objectives of the subject and to look at issues such as assessment expectations, possibilities for integration, teaching strategies, and specific information literacy concepts and skill sets.

Aside from the formal meetings, deliberate attention was paid to networking and remaining visible throughout the Faculty. The Faculty had always allocated its faculty librarian an office. This office was conveniently located near both the Dean's office and the Faculty's largest tea-room–two venues that were of course heavily utilized by staff! Each week, the Faculty Librarian would spend one morning in this office in order to take advantage of the opportunities it afforded to informally meet with staff, go to morning tea, and establish a working rapport with members of the Faculty of Education. Attending and presenting at Faculty planning days, faculty meetings, and other committee meetings was also a strategy employed as part of developing and promoting the program. Promotion is not the focus of this paper but was given much attention before and during implementation which began in full in 2001.

OVERVIEW OF THE DEVELOPED PROGRAM

The example provided is from the Health and Physical Education section and demonstrates what the program looks like for a pre-service student (see Table 1). For most semesters throughout their whole course of study, a targeted subject is listed along with the expected outcomes and types of skills to be covered. The language used reflects the influence of the Australian Information Literacy Standards. The next layer of the program is subject level (where detail about the subject and information literacy instruction is included). An example of this level is provided later in this article (refer to the example for EDIT102 under *Results*).

In essence the result was a tailored program for each main area of undergraduate study suited to the University of Wollongong's Faculty of Education particular needs. Nimon (2001) suggests this customized approach is a good one. She says that while the generic approach is (arguably) the best use of resources, the principles of successful information literacy skill development (cited in Haycock & Haycock 1984) include:

- context;
- understanding of the meaning and purpose of the skill;
- supervision to learn to avoid bad habits;
- the need for repeated opportunities;
- catering for individual help if needed;
- providing instruction at increasing levels of difficulty;
- generalizing at each stage so students can apply the skills learned in varied and different situations, therefore helping to make maximum transferability possible; and,
- flexibility in the instruction program so that skills can be taught as they are needed (45).

This program had many of these characteristics and was therefore open to success after implementation.

RESULTS

Since the implementation of the program in 2001 there have been a number of definable results.

Improved Outcomes for Students

Bodi (2002) says that undergraduate students often leave assignments until the last moment and quotes Leckie (1996) as saying that stu-

TABLE 1

Session	Subject	Outcomes	Skills
One	EDUF111 Education 1	• Identifies keywords, synonyms & related terms for the information needed • Constructs search strategies using appropriate commands (e.g., Boolean operators, truncation etc.) • Accesses a variety of reference sources relevant to information requirements (e.g., subject specific reference, Internet gateways, journals, etc.)	• Searching the Library Catalogue • Navigating the Subject resources & WebCT pages • Developing a search strategy
Two	EDIT102 Information Technology for Learning	• Differentiates between and values the variety of potential sources of information (e.g., people, databases, Web sites, etc.) • Explores general information sources to increase familiarity with the topic	• Navigating the Library's Web site • Basic Internet searching for information • Exploring Australia's Education Directory EdNA • Basic database searching • Interpreting database records
Three & Four	EDUP255 Teaching Physical Education & EDUP246 Risk Taking and Young People	• Develops a command of existing knowledge in a chosen discipline • Examines and compares information from various sources in order to critically evaluate reliability, validity, accuracy, authority, timeliness, and point of view or bias • Organizes the information to be used in a manner that supports the purposes and format of the product or performance • Communicates knowledge to others—spoken, written, graphic and other non-verbal forms appropriate to context	• Finding quality lesson plans • Locating policy documents for Education • Locating and evaluating Internet and other resources suitable for use in teaching • Using databases and resources from other subject areas/disciplines
Five	EDUP391 Research and Evaluation in Physical and Health Education	• Demonstrates an understanding of the research process and recognizes when more information is required • Identifies the intended purpose and audience of potential resources (e.g., popular vs. scholarly, current vs. historical) • Demonstrates an understanding of intellectual property, copyright, etc. • Uses specialized online or in person services to retrieve information needed (e.g., document delivery, professional associations, institutional research offices, community resources, experts & practitioners) • Communicates knowledge to others	• Using a broad range of information sources • Distinguishing between sources of information and developing deeper understanding of their structure and purpose (e.g., value of different search engines)

Session	Subject	Outcomes	Skills
Six	EDUP392 Social and Cultural Perspectives in Physical Activity and Phys Ed	• Constructs search strategies using appropriate commands (e.g., proximity operators, etc.) • Integrates prior and new knowledge • Communicates knowledge to others	• Advanced Database searching • Using more sophisticated search tools–e.g., Citation Indexes, Government papers, etc., when appropriate
Seven	EDUP453 Professional Studies in PE, PD and Health	• Identifies their existing knowledge framework • Articulates knowledge and skills transferred from prior experiences to planning and creating a product • Chooses a communication medium and format that best supports the purposes of the product or performance and the intended audience • Incorporates principles of design and communication appropriate to environment • Communicates clearly and with a style that supports the purposes of the intended audience	• Scanning for, and evaluating, appropriate related software packages • Developing awareness of the expectations on teachers for working with their School Librarian to integrate information literacy skills into their curriculum

dents have a "coping strategy, not an information-seeking strategy" (Bodi 2002, 110). Having an established program like this in place for undergraduates at least allows the *possibility* for good habit formation and more effective information-seeking practices to begin. In other words, the opportunity is there for students to develop lifelong learning competencies.

One of the experiential learning outcomes that students have gained from this program relates to the nature of finding information. Bodi (2002) says "Students rarely have so simple a search that they can follow the search strategy step-by-step and conclude with all the sources they need for an assignment. Instead, students, like scholars, hit deadends, need to backtrack, and need time to reflect on the information they have and what they still need . . . [However], scholars have the maturity to cope with the ambiguity and self-doubt inherent in research. They are gratified to find nothing written on their topic; students are devastated" (110). This is particularly true of undergraduates who just want to get the information as soon as possible and complete their assignments. This type of program shows that not always finding something does not mean giving up. There are repeated opportunities for students to learn that finding information is not always a straightforward process and that it often requires reflection and modification (not to mention patience). Some informal verbal feedback from students includes comments about feeling more confident to try again if their search fails the first time, and that they realize spending more time planning their search will often result in more effective retrieval of information.

Obvious Success Stories Promoting Information Literacy and the Benefits for Students

Undoubtedly one of the major successes in the implementation phase of this program was the work achieved in one of the core first year subjects called EDIT102, Information Technology for Learning. Being a core subject meant that this subject was compulsory for over 300 first-year students enrolled in any of the pre-service course degrees. To integrate information literacy into this subject the faculty librarian initially met with the subject coordinator, Christine Brown, to discuss the aims and objectives of the subject and to develop rapport and establish mutual goals. The subject aimed to provide students with the opportunity to learn and reflect on the role of information technology in learning and in the support it provided to the teacher. The design of the subject was around content and activities that got the students to learn about and reflect on their roles of learner, manager, designer and researcher. Each week a focus question–such as "How does the use of technology change your work in the classroom?"–was given to the students via the complementary WebCT site so that they could come to tutorials and lectures with some consideration given to a particular topic relating to the roles mentioned. The subject coordinator and faculty librarian spent much time considering the overlaps between information literacy and information technology and the ways in which these two could be perfectly integrated into this subject. All of the students had, by this stage, completed ILIP100 and engaged in some information literacy activities in another core subject offered the previous semester. Hence, the notion of providing opportunities for these pre-service students to build information literacy competence throughout the course was being practiced.

The faculty librarian and subject coordinator began the process by discussing appropriate resources which could be linked to each topic area. The next important consideration was about what the subject coordinator was hoping the students would learn at certain points. As this was a first-year subject, the emphasis would be on introducing small chunks at a time, giving the opportunity for students to build on their knowledge and skills at a non-threatening pace so their confidence could grow and the opportunity for support was always available. The information literacy skills and knowledge that were going to be included throughout the subject were then mapped to specific weeks where it was thought that the match between the content and skill could be best achieved within the safe learning environment the subject's design offered. Discussion then revolved around what teaching methodology to use in that particular week (e.g., face to face, online, team teaching). An example of what the plan looked like at this point is included in Table 2.

Detailed guides were then devised for students and, significantly, for the large team of tutors responsible for the nineteen weekly tutorial groups. Many of the tutors had expressed concern about their role in the information literacy instruction process. Some felt that the skills were new to them, and others felt that their skills were out-of-date. The guides were introduced at weekly meetings between the subject coordinator and the tutors to help overcome these concerns and provide for their learning as well.

By the end of the subject we felt confident that students would have had a supportive, learning environment to allow for significant enhancement of their skills and knowledge in information literacy and information technology. The students' results were the yardstick by which to measure this goal. The subject coordinator expressed "amazement" at the quality and depth of reflection expressed in a large number of the students' portfolio that comprised 40% of their assessment task. This portfolio involved completing a range of activities, one selected from a choice about each of the four roles of learner, manager, designer and researcher. For example, creating an annotated list of Web sites or performing an advanced search to locate a refereed article (detailing the search process and writing a critique of the retrieved item).

The work done in EDIT102 was widely promoted at Faculty and library-organized committee meetings (often through joint presentations between the faculty librarian and subject coordinator) and its success and sound pedagogy certainly helped get information literacy firmly placed on the faculty's agenda.

Increase in Class Numbers

Furthermore, as the program took off and good relationships developed with the academics in the Faculty, requests for classes "outside" the program increased–including a large and significant increase in the postgraduate and research student subjects.

TABLE 2

WK	FOCUS QUESTION	RESOURCES	INFO LIT
1	–		2nd Lecture Week 1 Introduce Database Concepts (building on EDUF111) Database demonstration Students to sign up for Database Tutorials in Weeks 5 & 6
2	*How does the technology change your work in the classroom?*	**Link to Subject Resources/Information Tech in Ed/Electronic Journals** **http://www.library.uow.edu.au/ Subjects/educres4.htm# E-Journals**	Students will: • Navigate through the link on the Library's Education Subject Resource Page on IT in Education to articles of relevance within a couple of e-journals • Discuss the articles in relation to the focus question • Bookmark the articles once they've located them
3	*How do you learn to use different kinds of technology? Tutorial to include search strategies for finding Web sites.*	**Link to Library's Internet Tutorial page** **http://www.library.uow.edu.au/ InfoServ/USE/int_tut.htm**	Students will be asked to: explore this page and select a tutorial to use (This will prepare them for later Internet searching and evaluation of Web sites.)
5 + 6	–	–	Hands-on database sessions in the Library

Better Scheduling for Faculty Librarian Possible

A useful benefit for the faculty librarian has been the ability to work with an information literacy schedule of classes. For example, the targeted subjects were the minimum number of classes to expect in a semester, and rather than waiting for the academic to make contact and establish class times (which can often occur at the last minute, due to heavy workloads and other responsibilities), the faculty librarian is able to make the first move and get things organized ahead of time. This is a valuable time management tool, especially at the hectic beginning of each session.

Other Results

Obviously not everything has worked well. One of the problems we have faced is called "gunghoism" by Andrea Glover in Chiste et al. (2000). In getting this program off the ground, the Acting Dean had been enormously helpful. Coupled with that, however, was perhaps over-ambition by both the Acting Dean and the faculty librarian. The program, for example, aimed to incorporate this comprehensive integration through all three main undergraduate programs at once. In practice, one program area took off much more slowly than the other two. One Director sensibly pointed out that perhaps focusing on development of one area at a time would have been a better approach. Related to this, of course, is the real issue of maintaining momentum. Keeping enthusiasm alive after implementation can be difficult.

Another unexpected result, as far as the faculty librarian was concerned, echoes Glover's statement: "Be aware that some of the opposition to information literacy initiatives may come from within your own ranks; your library colleagues may not be marching in time with you" (Chiste et al. 2000, 207). While the other faculty librarians in the team were all busy with their own information literacy classes and successes, the creation and development of this program did take an enormous amount of time and effort in the faculty and away from the Library. Feedback received from team members included comments about uneven workloads. For example, some colleagues in the Library felt that too much time was being allocated away from the other team responsibilities that the faculty librarian was expected to contribute to. While this certainly was not a deliberate outcome, it was a valid criticism. Faculty librarians with diverse and numerous responsibilities in Australian academic libraries are well aware that balancing the liaison role with internal Library responsibilities is a real challenge. Orr et al. (2001) have also noted this fact and add that maintaining momentum in the light of so many other responsibilities is particularly difficult.

One way around this is to utilize a strategy used at Central Queensland University, where the information literacy program was entirely delivered by the faculty responsible and the librarian acted as mentor (Orr et al. 2001, 458). It was certainly a deliberate strategy that the faculty librarian used in this instance by having the tutors so heavily involved in teaching the information literacy related sections of EDIT102. Of course there are other benefits–aside from time–of using this strategy. For example, it facilitates the development of information literacy development for both staff and students. In other situations it is a perfect way for real team teaching approaches, utilizing the expertise of both parties, to foster potently effective learning experiences.

In relation to this information literacy program, this strategy was used in a fourth-year Language subject (EDUL442) that is currently being offered. In this subject the students are introduced to research in the area of language education. By this stage of the program, students have already gained the skills to find relevant research articles and have a basic understanding of evaluation criteria. In one of their exercises for the subject, students are required to critique various research articles. The faculty librarian leads a discussion to reinforce the basic elements of evaluating information as applied to a particular article, and then the academic takes over to continue with the specific evaluation criteria relating to language research. This type of activity is often challenging and stimulating for students. As Grafstein (2002) points out: "In an IL program that is integrated into the academic curriculum, librarians and classroom faculty have complementary roles in the delivery of IL instruction" (201). She argues that academic staff and faculty librarians have complementary (though distinct) roles in helping students become information literate. It is the librarian who is uniquely qualified to teach the generic skills needed while the academic has the required discipline-specific knowledge. Orr et al. (2001) also make reference to this idea as it relates to Bruce's *seven faces* model which conceptualizes information literacy as seven inter-related components of: information technology conception, information sources conception, information process conception, information control conception, knowledge construction, knowledge extension conception and wisdom conception. She states: "The fact that these factors are interdependent emphasizes that the teaching of information literacy requires cooperation and knowledge of librarians and faculty in the design and delivery of programs" (Orr et al. 2001, 450). If we relate this to the EDUL442 example, we can see that the knowledge construction phase for the student is *assisted* by the librarian and academic in very important yet distinct ways.

DIRECTIONS

Academic libraries in Australia continue to be swept up in higher education and information environment changes, and they must rapidly adapt if they are to remain viable and essential institutions within their universities. Since implementation of this program, feedback and results have indicated the continuous need for improvement and flexibility. It was always intended that the program be a dynamic one—evolving and adapting to suit the needs of students and staff. The directions that are appearing at the present time revolve around the following themes (which are not listed in order of importance):

- Internationalization
- Information and Communication Technologies
- Research student needs
- Assessment
- Faculty changes
- Implementation of the Australian Information Literacy Standards.

INTERNATIONALIZATION

Internationalization is having a major impact on the University of Wollongong, as it is in other universities in Australia and abroad. International student enrollments are on the increase, and the University is actively pursuing international education markets around the globe. There is a large campus set up in Dubai, Saudi Arabia, and courses are being established in countries such as Malaysia, Singapore and Hong Kong. The University has also recently established campuses in Sydney, the South Coast, and Southern Highlands surrounding the Wollongong area to attract regional students to the University at locations nearer to their homes. The development of the libraries in these extended campuses is still in relatively early phases. There are no individual faculty librarians attached to these campuses, nor likely to be in the near future–particularly as arrangements have often been made with local TAFE (Technical and Further Education Colleges) and public libraries close to these campuses to provide basic library services and limited reference support.

Both the increase in international student enrollments and the spreading of campuses and course offerings by the University across the globe will undoubtedly become more significant in terms of information literacy instruction. Delivery options such as a specific online tutorial developed for our offshore commerce students by their faculty librarians is one example of a specific information literacy initiative. Developing and maintaining an information literacy program will require much more sophisticated collaboration and cooperation than what currently exists.

INFORMATION AND COMMUNICATION TECHNOLOGIES

WebCT has been implemented as the University's preferred online teaching and learning software. In response, the Faculty librarians have utilized this medium in various ways to incorporate information literacy instruction for on campus students where the WebCT has complemented face-to-face teaching or facilitated distance learning. Our Law librarians have developed specialized quizzes and other tools for their students who are using this medium. In the Faculty of Education, the faculty librarian has been working with staff to incorporate resources and instruction in programs such as EDIT102.

Use of other technologies and tools will need to be considered for inclusion in this information literacy program as they become part of the University's teaching and learning environment. As with the rapid developments taking place in the last couple of years, other developments will likely occur which will impact teaching and learning in ways that cannot be fully anticipated at this time. Of course, students' understanding and use of technologies are also changing, and these factors will need to be considered as well.

RESEARCH STUDENT NEEDS

It was mentioned earlier that as the program took off and good relationships developed with the academics in the Faculty, requests for classes "outside" the program increased, including a large and significant increase in the postgraduate and research student subjects. The University of Wollongong has succeeded in attaining a reputation as a University renowned for research excellence. The funding provided to the University in relation to its size is significant and impressive. The Library's vision, mission and values aim to support this and empower research students and staff to become competent lifelong learners.

To support this aim within the Faculty of Education, the faculty librarian has also been running a significant number of classes focusing on current resources and advanced skills for students and staff undertaking research method subjects. These continue to be heavily requested and attended. Since 2001 a series of hands-on workshops on topics such as finding theses, accessing e-journals, establishing journal alerts, and using EndNote have been included in the Faculty's Research Seminar series that are held every semester. These are well attended by research students and academic staff and have received very positive evaluations.

It is appropriate that the work being done with the postgraduate and research students be formally incorporated into this existing pre-service information literacy program in the near future.

ASSESSMENT

The area of assessment is one that has generated a great deal of discussion in the information literacy arena, especially in relation to higher education. It is certainly one of the areas of this comprehensive information literacy program that needs much greater attention and improvement. While some of the targeted subjects have assessable information-literacy activities attached to them, there needs to be a better approach to evaluating this program over the course of a student's study.

Pausch and Popp (1997) accurately claim that assessment must be done which shows that the cognitive concepts and skills being learned are necessary to other learning experiences if support from library administrators, campus administration, faculty and students is to be gained. Todd (2000) agrees with this view and suggests that investigation into the relationship between information literacy and independent learning and lifelong learning and an exploration of the outcomes and benefits derived from information literacy initiatives need to be performed in order to find out more from the student's perspectives and outcomes.

Seamans (2002) says that "without knowing much about how students obtain information or how they effectively use it makes it difficult to design instructional programs and provide services that are relevant to students" (112). She also says that we make many assumptions about first-year students in relation to their information seeking skills and knowledge and their use of information. Fisch (1999) reminds us that when considering the students' perspectives, the different student groups need to be taken into consideration (i.e., undergraduate, postgraduate, distance education students, English as second language students, etc.). This is an area that is receiving increased interest and is one that needs to be examined further.

Pausch and Popp (1997) also claim that assessment of information literacy programs should ideally include longitudinal studies. At the University of Wollongong the Health and Behavioural Sciences Faculty Librarian, Chris Brewer, performed such a longitudinal study of an information literacy program she conducted in a first year nursing subject. While the quantitative data from the study was inconclusive, qualitative feedback was largely positive and students felt that the program had supported their learning (Brewer 1999). Such a thorough and detailed assessment of this program has not yet been carried out but would certainly be invaluable in determining future directions of the program.

Indeed, devising an appropriate assessment strategy for this program probably requires there to be a compilation of several approaches. Fisch (1999) proposes a stakeholder model for evaluating information literacy programs that considers questioning managers, academic staff, library staff, and students. This model considers the relevance of the program from all viewpoints which impact the different stakeholder groups. From the administration's perspective, for example, it might include consideration of the relevance of the program to the institution's goals and objectives.

FACULTY CHANGES

The subjects and courses being offered by the Faculty continue to grow and change with time. Short term or tailored courses, for example, are on the increase. Program directors and subject coordinators change, and there are numerous other academic staff changes as well as people come and go and take study leaves or are absent for other reasons. It is essential that the program take into account these changes and remain flexible enough to adapt to the changing needs of the Faculty and students.

Since many of these changes have occurred since the original development of the program and its implementation, a re-examination of the program in consultation and discussion with current staff should take place. This would also serve to re-promote the program, allow for broader reflection on the program's success and failures (including those students who have been in the program for a couple of years), and consider fresh perspectives for the future.

IMPLEMENTATION OF THE AUSTRALIAN INFORMATION LITERACY STANDARDS

The final area that will influence the future directions of the program is in relation to the implementation of the Australian Information Literacy Standards. These Standards are currently being endorsed within University of Wollongong policy documentation relating to tertiary literacies. In 2001, the first edition of these Standards was endorsed and published by the Council of Australian University Librarians (CAUL). A national workshop to begin further revision of these Standards for the

Australian and New Zealand context took place in January 2003. Obviously, there may be implications for this information literacy program which will need to be considered in future developments.

CONCLUSION

This program began with the ultimate aim of ensuring that pre-service Education students in the Faculty of Education at the University of Wollongong were provided the opportunity for information literacy development throughout their course and at stages appropriate to their evolving roles of new university students, future teachers, and prospective postgraduate students. The enormous effort required to develop and implement a program to suit the ever-changing needs of students and staff within the higher education environment is just the beginning. It is an ongoing process that requires flexibility and commitment. While there are many indisputable advantages in offering a tailored, comprehensive approach, inevitable problems or "failures" arise. Constant evaluation is mandatory as is being able to successfully deal with the inevitable setbacks and changes that occur. Being proactive partners in the University's goal to foster graduates equipped with lifelong learning and information literacy competencies is nevertheless a crucial and rewarding role that librarians are expertly equipped to play. In the case of pre-service education students, a program such as this one that facilitates information literacy development among our future teachers who will, in turn foster such capacities in the next generation, is a challenging yet worthwhile venture. At the University of Wollongong we believe we are giving our students a flying start. The rest of their journey will be up to them.

REFERENCES

Bodi, Sonia. 2002. How do we bridge the gap between what we teach and what they do? Some thoughts on the place of questions in the process of research. *The Journal of Academic Librarianship* 28 (3): 109-114.

Brewer, Chris. 1999. Longitudinal study of an information literacy program at the University of Wollongong. In D. Booker (Ed.), *Concept, challenge, conundrum: From library skills to information literacy: Proceedings of the Fourth National Information Literacy Conference conducted by the University of South Australia Library and the Australian Library and Information Association Information Literacy Special Interest Group, 3-5 December 1999* (pp. 66-75). Adelaide: University of South Australia.

Bruce, Christine. 2000. Information literacy programs and research: An international review. *The Australian Library Journal* 49 (3): 209-218.

Bundy, Alan. 1999. Information literacy: The 21st century educational smartcard. *Australian Academic and Research Libraries* 30: 233-250.

Carr, Jo Ann. 1998. *Information literacy and teacher education* [online]. Washington, DC: ERIC Clearinghouse on Teaching and Teacher Education. (ERIC Document Reproduction Service No. ED 424231) [cited 5 March 2003]. Available World Wide Web: <http://www.ericfacility.net/ericdigests/ed424231.html>.

Council of Australian University Librarians (CAUL). 2001. *Information literacy standards*. Canberra: Council of Australian Information Literacy Standards.

Chiste, Katherine Beaty, Andrea Glover, and Glenna Westwood. 2000. Infiltration and entrenchment: Capturing and securing information literacy territory in academe. *The Journal of Academic Librarianship* 26 (3): 202-208.

Fisch, Eva (with Rosemary Cotter, David Cunnington and Barbara Paton). 1999. CRIG Annual User Education Seminar. Secret Librarian's Business: Positioning Information Literacy Practice.

Grafstein, Ann. 2002. A discipline-based approach to information literacy. *The Journal of Academic Librarianship* 28 (4): 197-204.

Langford, Linda. 2002. Information literacy–whose view, whose responsibility and does it really matter? *Access* 16 (3): 21-24.

Lipu, Suzanne, and Beth Peisley. 2001. Keeping our academics on the cutting edge: The academic outreach program at the University of Wollongong Library. *Revelling in Reference 2001 Reference and Information Services Section Symposium Proceedings 12-14 October 2001* (pp. 99-102).

McGurk, C. 1997. A curriculum-integrated approach to comprehensive information literacies. Project Report, University of Wollongong.

MacDonald, Mary C., Andree J. Rathemacher, and Joanna M. Burkhardt. 2000. Challenges in building an incremental, multi-year information literacy plan. *Reference Services Review* 28 (3): 240-247.

Nimon, Maureen. 2001. The role of academic libraries in the development of the information literate student: The interface between librarian, academic and other stakeholders. *Australian Academic and Research Libraries* 32 (1): 43-52.

Orr, Debbie, Margaret Appleton, and Margie Wallin. 2001. Information literacy and flexible delivery: Creating a conceptual framework and model. *The Journal of Academic Librarianship* 27 (6): 457-463.

Pausch, Lois M., and Mary Pagliero Popp. 1997. *Assessment of information literacy: Lessons from the higher education assessment movement* [online]. Chicago: Association of College & Research Libraries [cited 5 March 2003]. Available World Wide Web: <http://www.ala.org/acrl/paperhtm/d30.html>.

Seamans, Nancy H. 2002. Student perceptions of information literacy: Insights for librarians. *Reference Services Review* 30 (2): 112-123.

Todd, Ross. 2000. Information literacy: Concept, conundrum, and challenge. In D. Booker (Ed.), *Concept, challenge, conundrum: From library skills to information literacy: Proceedings of the Fourth National Information Literacy Conference conducted by the University of South Australia Library and the Australian Library and Information Association Information Literacy Special Interest Group, 3-5 December 1999* (pp. 25-34). Adelaide: University of South Australia.

Teaching Teachers to Teach: Collaborating with a University Education Department to Teach Skills in Information Literacy Pedagogy

Steve W. Witt

Julia B. Dickinson

SUMMARY. In June 2000, the Illinois State Board of Education adopted new state standards for all accredited teacher education programs. Professional certification programs must demonstrate compliance to the standards by July 2003. Library faculty at Illinois Wesleyan University partnered with the Educational Studies department to address the Core Technology Standards for information access, research, and information literacy through curriculum development. The program includes a combination of an information literacy pre-test, a self-paced, open source Web tutorial, traditional library instruction sessions, one-on-one student-librarian consultations with student teachers, and collaborative course design. The overall goal of the program is to improve librarian-teacher cooperation through instruction in the information literacy skills outlined in the In-

Steve W. Witt is Assistant Professor and Information Services Librarian, Illinois Wesleyan University, Bloomington, IL (E-mail: switt@iwu.edu).

Julia B. Dickinson is Assistant Professor and Public Services Librarian, Illinois Wesleyan University, Bloomington, IL (E-mail: jdickins@iwu.edu).

[Haworth co-indexing entry note]: "Teaching Teachers to Teach: Collaborating with a University Education Department to Teach Skills in Information Literacy Pedagogy." Witt, Steve W., and Julia B. Dickinson. Co-published simultaneously in *Behavioral & Social Sciences Librarian* (The Haworth Information Press, an imprint of The Haworth Press, Inc.) Vol. 22, No. 1, 2003, pp. 75-95; and: *Information Literacy Instruction for Educators: Professional Knowledge for an Information Age* (ed: Dawn M. Shinew, and Scott Walter) The Haworth Information Press, an imprint of The Haworth Press, Inc., 2003, pp. 75-95. Single or multiple copies of this article are available for a fee from The Haworth Document Delivery Service [1-800-HAWORTH, 9:00 a.m. - 5:00 p.m. (EST). E-mail address: docdelivery@haworthpress.com].

formation Literacy Competency Standards for Higher Education, and to mentor pre-service teachers in practical methods of integrating information literacy instruction in both their student teaching and their future professional lives. *[Article copies available for a fee from The Haworth Document Delivery Service: 1-800-HAWORTH. E-mail address: <docdelivery@haworthpress. com> Website: <http://www.HaworthPress.com> © 2003 by The Haworth Press, Inc. All rights reserved.]*

KEYWORDS. Information literacy, teacher education, collaboration with faculty, curriculum development, state standards

In June 2000, the Illinois State Board of Education adopted new curriculum standards for all accredited teacher education programs. The *Content-Area Standards for Educators* serve as a guideline for teacher preparation programs, accreditation criteria, and the groundwork for assessment of teachers in the state of Illinois. Professional programs must demonstrate compliance to the standards by July 2003. This case study provides an overview of Illinois' progress toward a standards-led model and describes how Illinois Wesleyan University library faculty initiated a collaborative project with the Educational Studies department to address information literacy skills instruction as a means of fulfilling objectives of the state's core standards. The overall goal of the program is to improve librarian-teacher cooperation through instruction in the information literacy skills outlined in the Information Literacy Competency Standards for Higher Education, and to mentor pre-service teachers in practical methods of integrating information literacy instruction in both their student teaching and their future professional lives.

LITERATURE REVIEW

Teacher education programs and library instruction have had an historical relationship that dates back to at least the late nineteenth century. As noted by O'Hanlon (1988a), this historical link provides both a context from which to view our current instruction programs and the realization that there has been a "continuing struggle to establish library instruction programs for future teachers" (528). Reviewing the literature from the late nineteenth and early twentieth century, one can see clearly that this "struggle" is influenced by two agents which tend to lead librarians and educators toward new approaches to teacher education in what we currently refer to as Information Literacy skills: technology and pedagogical skills.

First, one is struck with the fact that the advent of new technologies and easier access to increasing amounts of information from diverse sources has historically been a driving force behind the argument for more comprehensive instruction programs for pre-service teachers. A century ago, when increasingly sophisticated print indexes were the technology of the day, and libraries of all types were rapidly growing in number, Sturges (1910) commented that "the remarkable progress in the last decade . . . has brought the library with its countless volumes within easy reach . . . [and] if the library is to become a real power . . . all must be taught how to use it" (1003). One needs only to change the nouns used to describe the technology, and Sturges' spirited call to action would have been fitting in the 1980s with the influx of CD-ROM media and currently during the decade-long move into the Internet realm.

Amid the angst and opportunity brought on by over a century of rapid progress in our society's ability to create, categorize, and disseminate information, the need for and advocacy of bibliographic instruction for pre-service teachers has been a consistent pulse in the literature. Like the familiar echo of Sturges' voice, this literature too retells a similar story. The NEA's 1915 "Report on the Committee on Standardizing the Course of Study in Library Instruction in Normal Schools" argues that teachers need to know how to use libraries in order to teach their pupils library skills, and lists the essential skills that teachers need, including the use of library resources and the ability to evaluate and present children's literature. Harris (1934) describes the state of instruction programs at the time and offers for consideration a model program of instruction to be adopted by teachers' colleges. This fully developed program consists of 72 classroom hours and focuses mainly on the teaching of library skills to aid future teachers in furthering their studies in education and their fields of specialization and to select appropriate materials for their students. What these curricula had in common is that they taught pre-service teachers to use libraries and their resources to aid in their professional development and provided a framework from which to select and interpret children's literature. The stated goal of these curricula, however, was traditionally much more ambitious. Adams (1898) makes this quite clear: "Before training in the use of libraries and reference-books can form a part of the school system it is evident that teachers must be prepared to give such instruction" (84). It is clear then that the underlying assumption of these programs was that knowledge of libraries and their use would automatically synthesize with their pedagogical training, preparing new teachers to both create assignments that use the library at developmentally appropriate levels and promote the teaching of research skills.

By the mid-twentieth century, the library instruction community actively questioned the effectiveness of this type of curriculum. The education and library literature of this period contains a plethora of articles, which lament the inability of teachers to create assignments that appropriately teach and use library resources (Perkins 1965). These criticisms typically bemoan poorly planned assignments, which either overtax a school library's resources or require research and resources typical of graduate students. Again, this is a very familiar theme. One which suggests that teaching pre-service teachers to do graduate and undergraduate level research doesn't necessarily provide them with any pedagogical context with which to go forward and design appropriate assignments that teach children to use and interpret resources in a school library.

By the 1980s, a number of successful initiatives worked towards addressing the issues related to bridging the gaps in the library instruction received by pre-service teachers and pedagogical practice of teachers in the field (O'Hanlon 1987; Sheppard 1982; Tierno and Lee 1983). In many ways, projects such as these were a part of the overall movement away from the isolation of bibliographic instruction programs to the more integrated and collaborative approach to library instruction, which was re-packaged as information literacy instruction. These collaborative projects have had the effect of moving the instruction of pre-service teachers from teaching resource and behavior based skills to process-based teaching with the intention of informing future pedagogy. By teaching process as it relates to pedagogy rather than skills as they relate to a student's current and future research in education, these library instruction programs have shifted from being an appendage that supports the overall curriculum to a department-based program with the same pedagogical mission of teaching pre-service teachers to teach.

Although librarians and their new faculty collaborators laid the groundwork for improved teaching and student learning, the innovative bibliographic instruction programs described by Jacobson (1988) and information literacy programs described by Carr (1998) represent a patchwork of success that has yet to be completed. One of the primary reasons that programs such as this are not yet the norm is the fact that the role of the library in providing instruction in critical competencies such as research and critical thinking has gone largely unnoticed by the national and statewide bodies that enact and implement the educational and teaching standards that are often the impetus behind the curricula of teacher education programs. For example, in Illinois, a 1988 study of the coursework required of teaching certificates "found no direct references to instruction in the role of the school library, with the exception of requirements pertaining to . . . school library media personnel" (Jacobson 1988, 53). Just as technological changes led to increased availability of information and subsequent calls for including library instruction in teacher training programs, the rapid development of digital information technologies is leading States and other external agents of change within education to include information literacy and technology literacy in their new teaching standards. Through these changes, librarians are well prepared to aid their colleagues in meeting the challenges posed by these external standards.

UNIVERSITY AND SETTING

Illinois Wesleyan University (IWU) is an independent, undergraduate university with a student population of approximately 2,000. The University is organized around a College of Liberal Arts with professional programs in the College of Fine Arts, and School of Nursing. The College of Liberal Arts offers 39 majors and three pre-professional programs: Medical Technology, Pre-dental, and Pre-engineering. The College of Fine Arts includes the Schools of Art, Music, and Theatre Arts, and an interdisciplinary major in Music and Theatre. The School of Nursing offers a 4-year program and confers a Bachelor of Science in Nursing degree. As stated in its mission statement, the University strives to provide a liberal education of high quality, fostering values and skills that will sustain students over a lifetime of learning. For the past two years, the University has been preparing for a re-accreditation visit, so the area of assessment is of great interest to many campus constituents.

The Educational Studies Department has five full-time faculty with one additional position fulfilling both a teaching and a field placement coordinator role. The department also has three part-time adjunct faculty. The departmental curriculum supports elementary, secondary, and music education certification requirements. In addition to the teacher preparation program, Educational Studies also offers a major and a minor for non-teachers which draw upon multidisciplinary courses in psychology, political science, sociology, economics, history, anthropology, and women's studies. According to the Title II report for IWU, 86 students were admitted into the teacher education program for the 2000-2001 academic year; 47 of those students were engaged in the student teaching practicum which averages 30 hours per week for 16 weeks. Because the Educational Studies Department is firmly aligned with the mission of liberal arts learning, education students are expected to think critically, possess intellectual curiosity, be self-directed, and preserve the ethics of the teaching profession as they build content knowledge and apply educational philosophies and theories to practice. These attributes form the cornerstone of information literacy and lifelong learning.

The IWU library supports the University's teaching mission through a model of integrating information literacy skills into the disciplines through partnerships with library and teaching faculty. Research and information literacy skills are taught to students through curriculum-based instruction and collaboration with departments and their faculty. Much of this collaborative work has been through a successful library liaison program by which library faculty have worked with departments to coordinate collection development and support the curriculum through library instruction sessions. The teaching done by librarians within their liaison departments has, for the most part, followed the traditional model of working with a class for one or two sessions to teach a specific set of skills that support an assignment. Generally, these sessions have become integrated into a course or are initiated at the request of the teaching faculty.

Within this instruction program, most of the librarian-to-student contact takes place early in a student's college career within the campus' first-year-experience course, which is taught by faculty from across the campus. Although instruction provided through this program is highly regarded on campus, the library faculty determined that a stronger emphasis on the development of information literacy skills throughout the college experience, rather than through a first-year program alone, was needed to improve student performance and help to foster the acquisition of knowledge as students progress further into their fields of study. Particular emphasis needed to be placed upon the developmental nature of certain skills such as critical thinking and synthesis. For the past several years, the library at IWU has been working to revise its instruction program to include a stronger collaborative relationship between library liaisons and their departments to work towards the goal of integrating department-specific information literacy outcomes for different stages of a program. In order to implement a program that relies more upon librarian-to-teaching faculty collaboration at the classroom and departmental level, library faculty have worked to gain experience and expertise in areas such as course design and outcomes assessment.

In the spring of 2001, the IWU library was selected to join the Association of College and Research Libraries' information literacy assessment project titled, *Assessing Student Learning Outcomes in Information Literacy Programs: Training Academic Librarians*. The purpose of this project, which was funded through a grant from the Institute of Museum and Library Services, was to "give librarians the skills to create baseline data that supports the merits of information literacy programs . . . [by providing] training for academic librarians to work with faculty to design, implement, and evaluate tools for assessing student learning outcomes" (Association of College and Research Libraries Consultants for Information Literacy 2003). Through this grant, the Information Services Librarian worked with the Chair of the Educational Studies Department to develop a set of assessment tools for a Gateway course, the first-year-experience course that is designed to teach skills in writing and critical thinking. Together they worked to create a multi-staged writing and research assignment with a set of assessment tools that would qualitatively measure both student performance on an assignment and student outcomes in the information literacy skills taught in a series of three instruction sessions.

Through this successful collaboration, the Chair of the Education Studies Department learned more about how the library could support his department's efforts to adapt to the rigorous and outcomes-based standards being imposed by the state. Particularly, the project brought the library's potential role of delivering and coordinating content specifically related to information literacy to the department's attention when the process of adapting to the standards began.

ILLINOIS STATE STANDARDS

Although academic librarians have only recently seen a standards-based approach to educational objectives sweep the field, a culture of standards and assessment has long been the norm in primary and secondary public education (Arp 2002). The gap between standards for K-12 education and those for students in higher education is closing now that regional accreditation associations are specifically identifying information literacy as part of desired student learning outcomes (Gratch-Lindauer 2002). Illinois' educators began to address issues raised by the 1983 *Nation at Risk* report by designing *State Goals for Learning* in 1985. Over the next decade, various national research, federal education reforms, and state experiences indicated that the thirty-four Illinois goals needed substantial revision. In 1997, the *Illinois Learning Standards* (ILS) were adopted. These standards focus on student proficiencies in seven curricular areas, identifying goals, knowledge and skill indicators, and benchmarks. The Illinois State Board of Education funded a four-year study conducted by the University of Illinois at Urbana-Champaign to evaluate the implementation of the standards using a framework of five levels. DeStefano and Prestine (2002) reported that "[s]chools in the state are exhibiting strong evidence of transition to a standards-led system (Level Three), in most, if not all dimensions of implementation." The final report also noted that Level Three schools' principals and teachers "do not either have a clear sense of how to further ILS implementation or a strong desire to do so" (4). In addition to assessing progress toward full implementation of the *Illinois Learning Standards*, the evaluation indicated areas that prohibited implementation as well. Although district and school curricula had been aligned with the standards, classroom instruction methods had not substantially changed. Another problematic area identified by the study's survey data was that new teachers beginning their careers were not familiar enough with the standards.

These challenges to realization of a standards-led educational system echoed comments made by the Joint Education Committee of the State Board of Education and the Board of Higher Education in 1995. In the document entitled, *Illinois Framework for Restructuring the Recruitment, Preparation, Licensure and Continuing Professional Development of Teachers*, the Illinois teacher education system was described as "complex and inconsistent, marked by curriculum requirements that are not aligned with the knowledge and skills needed by classroom teachers" (Joint Education Committee 1996, 1). It was also noted that Illinois was one of few states that provided no requirements or incentives for continuing professional development for teachers. The Committee recommended that teaching standards must be designed to reflect the *Illinois Learning Standards* for students, directly tying teacher preparation to the state's education goals. In response, the *Illinois Professional Teaching Standards* were written into the Illinois Administrative Code in 1999. As Illinois continued to follow the national teacher preparation reform movement, these pedagogical standards were combined with content areas standards in language arts, technology and special education to form the core competencies for Illinois teachers. The document entitled *Content-Area Standards for Educators*, adopted in June 2000, and revised in October 2001, provides full details of the core standards as well as those developed for the various teaching fields and school administrators. These standards are aligned with the National Council for Accreditation of Teacher Education unit standards adopted in 2000.

In compliance with the federal *No Child Left Behind Act of 2001* (P.L. 107-110), the Illinois State Board of Education adopted the definition of a "highly qualified teacher" particularly as it pertains to state initiatives to improve teacher preparation programs, certification, and licensure. Illinois has restructured its Title II report card and is enacting laws that will require students to pass basic skills tests before being admitted to teacher preparation programs and to pass subject content exams before beginning the student teaching practicum. In addition, the implementation of the Assessment of Professional Teaching exam will begin in October 2003. It is designed to evaluate pre-service teachers on the Illinois Professional Teaching Standards, and the core language arts and technology standards. Teacher candidates must pass this exam before being issued the Initial Certificate.

The *No Child Left Behind Act* defines a "highly qualified teacher" as one who has a bachelor's degree, obtained state certification, and holds a state license to teach. The law will discontinue the current practice of hiring teachers without full certification through waivers. The definition emphasizes the importance of subject content knowledge, but includes reference to demonstrated teaching skills in the areas in which one teaches. The *Illinois Framework* document and the *Illinois Professional Teaching Standards* do not separate what a teacher knows from what a teacher can do; following the premise stated in *What Matters Most: Teaching for America's Future*, both in conjunction with each other comprise the state's interpretation of what it means to be the best teacher. Consequently, the importance of professional development for teachers figures heavily into Illinois' current standards-led reform. Updating subject knowledge and developing teaching skills firmly position teachers as lifelong learners. There is a general consensus among educators and researchers that a teacher who is information literate is better equipped to teach information literacy to students. While most teacher educators agree that higher order skills including critical thinking and problem-solving are most important for teachers, exactly how those skills are acquired and whose responsibility the building of those skills actually is has been an area of disagreement (O'Hanlon 1988b). As information literacy program development began to transform traditional library instruction efforts, discussion, exploration, and experimentation with regard to this issue ensued. Best practices research is now indicating that the responsibility for information literacy instruction lies not in one single domain, but that it requires cooperation and collaboration.

PROGRAM DESCRIPTION

The Illinois State Standards make little distinction between technology literacy and information literacy, creating the potential for programs that either focus primarily on technology training or information literacy instruction. Fortunately, due to the strong relationship between the library and the campus Information Technology Department, which supports technology training on campus, there was no struggle for one group to dominate the program. Both groups were able to work with the Educational Studies Department and communicate ways in which to divide the instruction and integrate both skill areas into the curriculum.

The Educational Studies Department and the IT Department designed a series of hardware and software workshops for the education students. Since the core technology standards emphasize the importance of teaching with technology in the classroom, the focus of this training is not merely the technology skills, but their application in an educational setting. The technology tutorials were developed to cover various pieces of hardware, application software, and the Internet as a classroom communication and teaching tool. To augment the IT Department's instruction, the campus contracted a site license for a nationally recognized Web-based technology training program. At this writing, the IT Department is implementing a program that will allow this self-paced tutorial package to address the disparate technology competencies of undergraduate students while also serving to act as a bridge toward students' ability to develop pedagogically appropriate assignments that use information technology.

While the IT Department's focus is on bringing each student to a high level of technological competency and teaching pre-service teachers ways in which to use the technology to improve their future instruction, the librarians interpreted their role in supporting the adherence to the standards as teaching pre-service teachers to teach information literacy skills. This required an ambitious vision of a collaboration in which education faculty integrate information literacy into the curriculum to develop the skills and the librarians teach and mentor students in the theory and practice of information literacy instruction. The aim of this program is not only to support librarian-teacher cooperation at the K-12 level but to also encourage information literacy instruction to move beyond the libraries and media centers and into a synergistic environment.

With the education department's interest in some form of collaboration firmly established, the Information Services Librarian and the Public Services Librarian, who has a liaison role to the Educational Studies

Department, arranged a meeting with the department chair in order to discuss ways that the library could assist in meeting the new objectives for student learning. Armed with the core technology standards from the *Content-Area Standards for Educators,* the librarians prepared for this meeting by extracting knowledge and performance indicators that had correlates to the ACRL Information Literacy Standards (Appendix). Many process-based components of research skills had been embedded in a variety of the state standards. The distinction between technological competency and information literacy was often blurred in the language of the standards. The chair initially proposed a handful of sessions that were to be delivered by a librarian outside of scheduled class time. The sessions described to the library faculty at this first meeting included the history of technology, copyright and ethics of technology use, evaluation of information, and online searching. The librarians began negotiating for a more integrated and developmental approach. The chair was interested in the ideas presented, but expressed concern about sacrificing class time for what was still assumed to be a series of library instruction sessions. Prepared for this response, the librarians inquired about discussions that had happened within the department as well as the education students' responses to the new requirements. The dialogue that ensued established shared definitions of terminology, identified common student learning goals, and provided a framework within which to collaboratively address the concerns the rapid curricular reform raised. Both librarians and education faculty decided that the first step would be to target one sophomore class, one junior class, and the student teaching seminar occurring fall semester.

Three primary concerns surfaced during these meetings with the education faculty. The students currently in the education program grappled with how they could possibly meet the rigorous requirements given the fact that the changes were implemented after they were part of the way through the major sequence. The librarians suggested using TILT, the Texas Information Literacy Tutorial, as one way to satisfy the expressed student desire to test out of certain workshops proposed to them by the department chair. Some education faculty felt that teaching to a test, or to a state standard, sacrificed the depth of knowledge and theoretical understanding that distinguishes one teacher education program from another. The self-paced nature of TILT addressed the teaching faculty's perception of too little class time to cover too much information. The Web-based tutorial was attractive to the librarians as well because it could serve as both an instructional and an assessment tool. The librarians' concern has consistently been with curricular integration and proving the value-added nature of information literacy instruction. The fact that TILT's measure of student performance could be a component of the required education student portfolio was an added bonus.

Adopting the use of TILT turned out to be a much slower process than the librarians had initially anticipated. The online tutorial required changes to the campus network and technology updates that are still forthcoming. This change required the librarians to adjust the initial implementation of TILT to a much more modest version that wouldn't allow data collection about student performance and perceptions of the tutorials. As an experimental alternative to using the outcomes of the TILT modules, the librarians did a limited test of an electronic pre- and post-test that was developed by Lewis and Clark College. Both the TILT modules and pre- and post-tests were modified and successfully piloted with two groups of first year students to ensure both test validity and positive student responses to the use of electronic tutorials and tests.

The initial coursework for education majors includes a cross-disciplinary theory course and a child development class. These classes are open to majors and non-majors. It is during the sophomore year that students formally apply to Illinois Wesleyan's teacher preparation program for professional certification. The Illinois state standards now require teacher candidates to pass an enhanced Basic Skills Test before admission to a teacher education program. The enhanced Basic Skills Test is aligned with the *Illinois Learning Standards* and reflects an expected college sophomore level competency in reading comprehension, language arts, mathematics, and a written essay.

The course, Studying Children and Adolescents in Context (Educ 255), is the first discipline-specific course in the major sequence. This class also provides education students with their first field experience. In fall of 2002, this course had less than half the expected enrollment. Plans made during the summer with regard to incorporating information literacy skills into specific class assignments were revised because of the necessity of restructuring the assignments based on enrollment numbers. The education liaison librarian designed a traditional library instruction session that would introduce the students to the ERIC Web site. The instructor had restructured the small class using an independent study model that culminated in a research paper based on secondary literature as well as the students' field experience. The librarian adapted the online ERIC PowerPoint tutorial using the students' individual topics and local holdings information to customize examples. In so doing, the librarian modeled the use of technology in the classroom and demonstrated how the presentation addressed the State's core technology standard regarding accessing and using information to improve teaching and learning.

After students are accepted into the teacher education program, they begin taking curriculum classes based on subject areas and grade level certification. Teaching Social Studies in Elementary School (Educ 315) exposes students to curriculum theory, lesson plan design, and assessment. The course lays the groundwork for the student teaching experience. The instructor planned the course this fall around migrant farm workers and asked the students to work in small groups to construct lesson plans for each of the social studies areas as an integrated unit using migrant labor as the focus. The librarian's presentation to this class concentrated on identifying tools and strategies to locate various resources with which to build lesson plans. Most of these students were not aware of teaching tools available to them via educational Web sites designed by and for teachers. Even fewer were knowledgeable about print resources including reference materials and government documents. The instructor requested that the students be given an introductory primer on copyright issues with regard to fair use and various formats, including print, images, sound, and Internet material. It became apparent that the majority of these students in the third year of the Educational Studies program were still fully immersed as student learners, not yet possessing strong independent-learning skills that would enable them to envision themselves as novice professionals.

The Illinois State Board of Education has stipulated that universities and colleges must demonstrate compliance to the new state standards by July 2003. Although the seniors engaged in the student teaching practicum this year are not expected to meet all the new requirements, arrangements were made in the summer to have the education library liaison be a guest speaker for the student teaching seminar which meets once a week. The instructor and librarian agreed that perhaps the most useful and applicable presentation would include detailed information about the limitations of copyright law's educational fair use and a basic toolkit to integrate information literacy and its assessment into classroom assignments. The librarian provided an overview of assignments constructed using Bloom's taxonomy, the Big 6 <http://www.big6.com/>, the Information Power standards (AASL 1998), and the "toolkit" provided in Ryan and Capra (2001).

The challenge continues to be integrating information literacy within the course assessment using a developmental approach over the four years of the University's teacher education program. The library faculty at IWU still find themselves having to clarify the distinction between the how-to instruction the Information Technology Department delivers and the more process-oriented instruction that the librarians are capable and desirous of integrating throughout the curriculum. Although the library faculty does its share of database demonstrations and the traditional nuts and bolts instruction, the attention to the enhancement of the information literacy program has shifted the educational goal toward facilitating student learning instead of attempting to deposit knowledge and dispense facts. As is repeated in the constructivist community, librarians like teachers strive to be not the sage on the stage, but the guide on the side. If this commonality of approach is recognized, the mission of producing lifelong learners through collaborative curricular planning will be secured. As Gratch-Lindauer (2002) concludes, "(T)he most direct contribution the library makes to institutional goals is its role in developing clear student learning objectives for information literacy skills; assessing the progress and achievement of these objectives; and showing how the outcomes are used to improve student learning" (19). It is the opinion of the authors that continued collaboration with the education faculty will result in a stronger ongoing measure of accountability and program effectiveness than the evaluation of the teacher candidates' student portfolio and student teaching experience might allow.

While initial discussions with the education faculty regarding collaborative course re-design have begun, a variety of factors have slowed the execution of this partnering goal, not the least of which was a resignation within the Educational Studies Department. The librarians are confident that the library, the Educational Studies Department, and the Information Technology Department have embarked upon a project that capitalizes on the expertise of various stakeholders in the university's educational mission. Best practice models identified in Dewey's *Library User Education: Powerful Learning, Powerful Partnerships* (2001) confirm that the librarians have positioned themselves strategically in order to facilitate further campus involvement with information literacy. According to departmental reports, the Educational Studies curriculum touches ten percent of IWU's student body. Non-majors are welcome in initial education courses and students anticipating certification for the secondary grades are drawn from a variety of disciplinary curricula, including History, English, Biology, Chemistry, Physics, Mathematics, and Modern and Classical Literatures and Languages. It is hoped that this level of diverse student participation will increase the grassroots outreach of the pilot project in conjunction with the library faculty's active involvement in the university's self-governance and strong liaison program. Interest has already piqued with the librarian who has a liaison role with the English Department because a significant number of students in the secondary education program seek certification in Language Arts.

The overall goal of the library's role in this developing program with the Educational Studies Department is to assist students in the teacher education program with the acquisition of information literacy skills as student learners and then facilitate their transition to teaching information literacy competencies to their future students as professional teachers. Because students are not formally admitted to the teacher education program until their junior year, the program's focus for the courses directed at students in the first and second years is on building information literacy competencies as student learners. Continued and expanded use of assessment tools will provide librarians and education faculty with a realistic picture of the level of skill beginning students have. From that data, the librarians will work with the education faculty to plot the trajectory of information literacy instruction through the end of the sophomore year. As the first-year experience Gateway Colloquia program is evaluated by an appointed taskforce of teaching faculty and the Information Services Librarian, perhaps student information literacy skills will stabilize and become more predictable. Until then, an attempt will be made to equalize student information literacy competencies through a combination of library instruction sessions, TILT, course assignments designed collaboratively by library and education faculty that integrate information literacy skills, and one-on-one research consultation appointments between a librarian and a student requiring individualized assistance. One possibility might be to coordinate assessment of sophomore level information literacy skills with scores on the State's enhanced Basic Skills Test that must be passed before formal admission to the teacher preparation program is granted.

The curriculum courses taken during the third year will allow students to practice evaluation and synthesis skills as immersion into subject content knowledge is used to design lesson plans. Guided exposure to standards-based assignments incorporating a variety of models, such as Big 6 and the Illinois School Media Specialists' workbook entitled, *Links for Learning*, will be provided through course integration and assignment development clinics to allow education students to work in an interactive group environment with the librarians. While the focus of these practice sessions will be on designing assignments around information literacy skills, incorporating the use of technology in assignments will also be encouraged. Although plans have not been formalized at this writing, requiring these junior level students to work with a school media specialist or a public librarian in the location of their field experience would foster a partnership with those who have knowledge of available resources and tools for school assignments. Initiating this contact early in the development of education students may assist them in the transition of perspective from college student to pre-service teacher.

The fourth and final year of the proposed program will be split between the student teaching practicum and the capstone course. While the majority of the education students at Illinois Wesleyan student teach in the fall, those students participating in the Urban Education Program and some students in the Music Education Program might student teach in the spring. Consequently, the proposed program needs to be flexible in its application and delivery. The student teaching seminar is designed to be reflective and student-driven, offering opportunities to address practical issues encountered in the field experience. Guest speakers, such as the Director of the Career Center, have been invited to the seminar in the past. It was within this established framework that the librarian became involved with the seminar in fall 2002. The current proposed program does not change this structure. One seminar session with the librarian will focus on lesson plan assessment examining classroom students' performance and recommending appropriate modifications. A second session will explore copyright law as it pertains to teachers and student assignments. Yet to be addressed, however, is the role the Educational Studies library liaison will have with the Music Education student teachers; preliminary discussions with the Fine Arts Librarian who has liaison responsibility to the School of Music have begun with the intention of developing a partnership that satisfies the needs of this unique group of pre-service educators.

Currently, the capstone course of Illinois Wesleyan's teacher education program is Issues in Educational Research and Practice (Educ 401). The course explores the connections among theory, practice, and research in the discipline. The course also helps students prepare the culmination of each education student's four years of study into an electronic portfolio which comprises part of the teacher candidate's assessment for certification. It is at this advanced level that the proposed program will incorporate problem-based learning scenarios to further demonstrate education student mastery of information literacy skills.

CONCLUSION

As described earlier, the challenges the librarians encountered during program development are familiar. Establishing a shared definition of information literacy can be a struggle, but having to negotiate an understanding within the terminology used in the state standards added a new layer of interpretation that needed to be addressed and satisfied. Given the immediacy of the need to restructure the Educational Studies curriculum, it was imperative that the librarians make a convincing argument that the library's role in teaching information literacy skills could be integrated into the curricular reform and need not be an add-on either through traditional library instruction or workshops outside of class time. Although there was early faculty support with regard to the library assisting the department in its efforts to address the state standards, it became apparent that any changes within the department in terms of personnel or responsibilities could in fact derail the progress the librarians had made with the teaching faculty individually. One challenge that is ongoing on the Illinois Wesleyan University campus, and that was somewhat unexpected in terms of collaboration with the Educational Studies Department specifically, is anticipation that assessment measures clash with intellectual freedom issues. Discussions with the department regarding the means used to evaluate the current proposed program's strengths and weaknesses will require sensitivity so that the library's vested interest will not give any weight to the concern that assessment is anathema to academic freedom by advocating prescriptive change and mandating evaluation from outside observers.

From the librarians' perspective, one of the strengths of this project with Educational Studies is that there are a number of measures that will be used to evaluate and shape the program through its full implementation. Because the departmental curriculum must respond to state boards and national accreditation agencies, the information literacy components are more likely to be seen as a fully integrated part of the curriculum and not merely a library initiative. The inherent nature of an education department is rich in terms of course design and assessment of teaching and of student performance. This environment provides the librarians with a forum from which to learn and to which to make significant contributions. Although the Illinois State Standards have been received with mixed feelings, the opportunity to collaborate allows experimentation with various learning models and instructional delivery methods. The new methodologies employed in this collaboration between the Educational Studies Department and the library will act as a campus-wide model and further the library's role in shepherding the development of the university's information literacy program. Sharing ownership of the issue of building information literacy skills will certainly go a long way toward producing a shared solution.

As July 2003 approaches and as feedback from the Illinois State Board of Education regarding the strengths and weaknesses of Illinois Wesleyan's teacher preparation program is addressed, the librarians are poised to revise the proposed information literacy program for education students. In pursuit of the next steps for this burgeoning program, the authors will strive to encourage interaction beyond the librarian-teaching faculty partnership on campus by seeking input from public librarians and school media specialists. Research in librarianship has only recently begun to explore means to close the K-12 and higher education information literacy skill gap. Initiatives such as the 1998 AASL/ACRL Task Force on the Educational Role of Libraries may foster further research that will change the face of information literacy programs as we currently know them.

REFERENCES

Adams, Emma Louise. 1898. Instruction in the use of reference-books and libraries. *Library Journal* 22: 84-86.

American Association of School Librarians and Association for Educational Communications and Technology. 1998. *Information power: Building partnerships for learning*. Chicago: American Library Association.

Arp, Lori, and Beth S. Woodard. 2002. Recent trends in information literacy and instruction. *Reference & User Services Quarterly* 42 (2): 124-32.

Association of College and Research Libraries Consultants for Information Literacy. *IMLS assessment grant home page*. [online]. Chicago: Association of College & Research Libraries [cited 3 January 2003]. Available from World Wide Web: <http://www.csusm.edu/acrl/imls/>.

Carr, Jo Ann. 1998. *Information literacy and teacher education* [online]. Washington, DC: ERIC Clearinghouse on Teaching and Teacher Education. (ERIC Document Reproduction Service No. ED 424231) [cited 5 March 2003]. Available World Wide Web: <http://www.ericfacility.net/ericdigests/ed424231.html>.

DeStefano, Lizanne, and Nona Prestine. 2002. *Report to the Illinois State Board of Education*. [online]. Springfield, IL: Illinois State Board of Education [cited 12 December, 2002]. Available from World Wide Web: <http://www.isbe.net/board/meetings/sept02meeting/ilssumrecom.pdf>.

Dewey, Barbara I. (Ed.). 2001. *Library user education: Powerful learning, powerful partnerships*. Lanham, MD: The Scarecrow Press.

Gratch-Lindauer, Bonnie. 2002. Comparing the regional accreditation standards: Outcomes assessment and other trends. *Journal of Academic Librarianship* 28 (1): 14-25.

Illinois State Board of Education. 1999. *The Illinois professional teaching and administrative standards taken from State Board's rule for certification (23 Ill. Adm. Code 25).* [online]. Springfield, IL: The Author [cited 12 December, 2002]. Available from World Wide Web: <http://www.isbe.net/recertification/CRManual%20PDFs/Word/tchgstds.doc>.

Illinois State Board of Education. 2001. *Title II–1998 Higher Education Act.* [online]. Springfield, IL: The Author [cited 17 December, 2002]. Available from World Wide Web: <http://www.isbe.net/nclb/csa/appendices/schrptcard.pdf>.

Illinois State Board of Education. Division of Professional Preparation. 2000. *Content area standards for educators: making Illinois schools second to none.* Springfield, IL: State of Illinois.

Jacobson, Frances F. 1988. Teachers and library awareness: Using bibliographic instruction in teacher preparation programs. *Reference Services Review* 16 (4): 51-5.

Joint Education Committee of the State Board of Education and the Board of Higher Education. 1996. *Illinois framework for restructuring the recruitment, preparation, licensure and continuing professional development of teachers.* [online]. Springfield, IL: Illinois State Board of Education [cited 17 December, 2002]. Available from World Wide Web: <http://www.isbe.net/profprep/PDFs/Framework1996.pdf>.

National Commission on Teaching and America's Future. 1996. *What matters most: Teaching for America's future.* New York: The Commission.

National Education Association. 1915. Report of the Committee on Standardizing the Course of Study in Library Instruction in Normal Schools. In *Addresses and Proceedings–National Education Association* 53: 1059-1064.

O'Hanlon, Nancy. 1987. Library skills, critical thinking, and the teacher-training curriculum. *College & Research Libraries* 48: 17-26.

O'Hanlon, Nancy. 1988a. Up the down staircase: Establishing library instruction programs for teachers. *RQ* 27: 528-34.

O'Hanlon, Nancy. 1988b. The role of library research instruction in developing teachers' problem solving skills. *Journal of Teacher Education* 39 (6): 44-49.

Perkins, Ralph. 1965. *Teacher's knowledge of library fundamentals.* New York: Scarecrow Press.

Ryan, Jenny, and Steph Capra. 2001. *Information literacy toolkit: Grades Kindergarten-6.* Chicago: American Library Association.

Sheppard, Jerry L. 1982. Establishing library skills proficiency in a teacher education program. *College and Research Libraries News* 43: 351-52.

Sturges, James V. 1910. The training of teachers in the use of books and the library and in a knowledge of children's books in *Addresses and Proceedings–National Education Association* 48: 1003-1013.

Tierno, Mark J., and Joann H. Lee. 1983. Developing and evaluating library research skills in education: A model for course-integrated bibliographic instruction. *RQ* 22: 284-91.

APPENDIX. Comparison of Illinois Core Technology Standards (2000) and Information Literacy Competency Standards (2000)

Illinois Core Technology	ACRL Information Literacy
Standard One *Basic Computer/Technology Operations and Concepts* The competent teacher will use computer systems to run software; to access, generate, and manipulate data; and to publish results. He or she will also evaluate performance of hardware and software components of computer systems and apply basic trouble-shooting strategies as needed.	Standard Two The information literate student accesses needed information effectively and efficiently. Standard Four The information literate student, individually or as a member of a group, uses information effectively to accomplish a specific purpose.
Standard Two *Personal and Professional Use of Technology* The competent teacher will apply tools for enhancing personal professional growth and productivity; will use technology in communicating, collaborating, conducting research, and solving problems and will promote equitable, ethical, and legal use of computer/technology resources.	Standard Two The information literate student accesses needed information effectively and efficiently. Standard Four The information literate student, individually or as a member of a group, uses information effectively to accomplish a specific purpose. Standard Five The information literate student understands many of the economic, legal, and social issues surrounding the use of information and accesses and uses information ethically and legally.
Standard Three *Application of Technology in Instruction* The competent teacher will apply learning technologies that support instruction in his or her grade level and subject areas. He or she must plan and deliver instructional units that integrate a variety of software, applications, and learning tools. Lessons developed must reflect effective grouping and assessment strategies for diverse populations.	Standard Four The information literate student, individually or as a member of a group, uses information effectively to accomplish a specific purpose. Standard Five The information literate student understands many of the economic, legal, and social issues surrounding the use of information and accesses and uses information ethically and legally.
Standard Four *Social, Ethical, and Human Issues* The competent teacher will apply concepts and skills in making decisions concerning the social, ethical, and human issues related to computing and technology. The competent teacher will understand the changes in information technologies, their effects on workplace and society, their potential to address life-long learning and workplace needs, and the consequences of misuse.	Standard Five The information literate student understands many of the economic, legal, and social issues surrounding the use of information and accesses and uses information ethically and legally.
Standard Five *Productivity Tools* The competent teacher will integrate advanced features of technology-based productivity tools to support instruction, extend communication outside the classroom, enhance classroom management, perform administrative routines more effectively, and become more productive in daily tasks.	Standard Three The information literate student evaluates information and its sources critically and incorporates selected information into his or her knowledge base and value system. Standard Four The information literate student, individually or as a member of a group, uses information effectively to accomplish a specific purpose.
Standard Six *Telecommunications and Information Access* The competent teacher will use telecommunications and information-access resources to support instruction.	Standard Two The information literate student accesses needed information effectively and efficiently. Standard Four The information literate student, individually or as a member of a group, uses information effectively to accomplish a specific purpose.

Illinois Core Technology	ACRL Information Literacy
Standard Seven *Research, Problem Solving, and Product Development* The competent teacher will use computers and other technologies in research, problem solving, and product development. The competent teacher will appropriately use a variety of media, presentation, and authoring packages; plan and participate in team and collaborative projects that require critical analysis and evaluation; and present products developed.	Standard Two The information literate student accesses needed information effectively and efficiently. Standard Three The information literate student evaluates information and its sources critically and incorporates selected information into his or her knowledge base and value system. Standard Four The information literate student, individually or as a member of a group, uses information effectively to accomplish a specific purpose.
Standard Eight *Information Literacy Skills* The competent teacher will develop information literacy skills to be able to access, evaluate, and use information to improve teaching and learning.	Standard One The information literate student determines the nature and extent of the information needed. Standard Two The information literate student accesses needed information effectively and efficiently. Standard Three The information literate student evaluates information and its sources critically and incorporates selected information into his or her knowledge base and value system. Standard Four The information literate student, individually or as a member of a group, uses information effectively to accomplish a specific purpose.

Survey of the Influence
of Mississippi School Library Programs
on Academic Achievement:
Implications for Administrator
Preparation Programs

Thelma Roberson
William Schweinle
Mary Beth Applin

SUMMARY. This article describes recent curricular changes being made to the Educational Administration program at the University of Southern Mississippi to include information regarding the value of quality school library programs and the effective management of such programs. Faculty involved in the course changes are also conducting a two-part study to determine the current status of public school libraries in Mississippi, their impact on academic achievement, and how the perceptions of teachers,

Thelma Roberson and William Schweinle are both Assistant Professors, Department of Educational Leadership and Research, University of Southern Mississippi, Hattiesburg, MS (E-mail: Thelma.Roberson@usm.edu or William.Schweinle@usm.edu).

Mary Beth Applin is Assistant Professor, University Libraries, University of Southern Mississippi, Hattiesburg, MS (E-mail: Mary.Applin@usm.edu).

[Haworth co-indexing entry note]: "Survey of the Influence of Mississippi School Library Programs on Academic Achievement: Implications for Administrator Preparation Programs." Roberson, Thelma, William Schweinle, and Mary Beth Applin. Co-published simultaneously in *Behavioral & Social Sciences Librarian* (The Haworth Information Press, an imprint of The Haworth Press, Inc.) Vol. 22, No. 1, 2003, pp. 97-114; and: *Information Literacy Instruction for Educators: Professional Knowledge for an Information Age* (ed: Dawn M. Shinew, and Scott Walter) The Haworth Information Press, an imprint of The Haworth Press, Inc., 2003, pp. 97-114. Single or multiple copies of this article are available for a fee from The Haworth Document Delivery Service [1-800-HAWORTH, 9:00 a.m. - 5:00 p.m. (EST). E-mail address: docdelivery@haworthpress.com].

Digital Object Identifier: 10.1300/J103v22n01_07   97 principals and librarians shape the function and use of those libraries. The results of the first phase of the study are described. *[Article copies available for a fee from The Haworth Document Delivery Service: 1-800-HAWORTH. E-mail address: <docdelivery@haworthpress.com> Website: <http://www.HaworthPress.com> © 2003 by The Haworth Press, Inc. All rights reserved.]*

KEYWORDS. School libraries, student achievement, school administrator preparation, Mississippi

For many, the school library is traditionally remembered as the place students went for study hall, film viewing, or baby-sitting when the classroom teacher was away from class. In the same respect, school librarians are remembered as 'keepers of the books,' 'shushers' who expected students to be seen but not heard while visiting the school's book sanctuary. Rarely is the school library or librarian remembered as an integral part of the learning experience. Given this mental model created by past experiences with school libraries, many in the field of education have failed to give credence to the notion that an active school library can actually have a positive effect on student achievement. Yet, there exists a significant body of research which indicates that effective school library programs can and do contribute to the overall academic success of students.

As early as the 1960s, researchers began amassing evidence that correlated higher student achievement with access to quality library services in the school setting. Of the many studies, some of the most significant have been published within the last 10 years and include the work of Lance (1994), Lance et al. (1999), Lance, Rodney and Hamilton-Pennell (2000a, 2000b), Baughman (2000), Smith (2001), and Rodney, Lance, and Hamilton-Pennell (2002). These empirically-based studies are particularly convincing because of their use of correlation and factor analytic methods to isolate specific characteristics of school library programs that contribute to academic achievement while controlling for other influences. These studies reported positive correlations between certain attributes of school library programs and higher scores for students on standardized tests. These specific library attributes include staffing levels; student/teacher access to the library; the librarian's level of collaboration and involvement with the curriculum and instruction; large, up-to-date collections; access to technology; and the school's partnership with the local public library.

IMPORTANCE OF ADMINISTRATIVE SUPPORT

The building-level principal has tremendous influence over the operations of the school and the overall school climate. His or her attitude and support of the school library program is one of the greatest determining factors of whether or not a school's library will have the attributes necessary to positively influence academic achievement (Charter 1982; Haycock 1999; Hellene 1973; AASL/AECT 1988; Oberg, Hay, & Henri 1999; Wilson & Lyders 2001). Decisions made by the principal regarding the budget, space utilization, technology, personnel/hiring, scheduling, assignment of duties, curriculum planning, committee appointments, etc., all have an impact upon school libraries (Hartzell 2002). In light of the important role the school library plays in student learning and the influence principals have in creating and sustaining quality library programs, it is imperative that principals have an awareness of the value of library programs and the role they play in student learning. Absent this knowledge, libraries may be viewed as a 'luxury' and/or a nonessential element in the school environment (Connors 1984). When such attitudes prevail and influence decision making, the school library becomes an easy target for budget cuts (Hartzell 2002).

With a collective budget shortfall of $50 billion in 2002 (Washington Post 2002), most states were forced to make major cuts in public programs including education. These cuts were passed on to the local school level where administrators were faced with the daunting task of eliminating and/or reducing student services. Unfortunately, many of these cuts occurred in library programs (Coeyman 2002).

NEED FOR ADMINISTRATOR TRAINING

Although past and current findings overwhelmingly support the notion that more effective school library programs increase student achievement, many administrators and classroom teachers still hold a stereotype of libraries as disposable. Hartzell (2002) in "What's it Take?" offered two reasons why this may be so: (1) the current age of our school leaders, and (2) lack of dissemination of school library research in education and school administration journals. Susan Gates, a Rand economist, reported at a National Forum on Education Policy that the average age of school principals in the year 2000 was 49.3 years (Anthes 2002). The National Center for Education Statistics reported that in 1998, 56% of professors in colleges of education were 50 or older (NCES 2001). That means that at least half of our school leaders and those who prepare future teachers and school administrators attended K-12 schools in the 1950s and 1960s. Most schools during this era had no centralized library and, therefore, lacked a professionally trained librarian. For the 1953-1954 school year, the U.S. Department of Education reported that only 38% of public schools in the United States had a centralized library (Wright 1960). By the 1962-1963 school year, that percentage had risen to only 59% and of those, less than half were supervised by a librarian with 15 or more hours of library training (American Library Association, 1965). By 1978 at least 85% of public schools had a library, yet less than a third of these had a librarian with a library-related degree (Cahalan 1987). During this early period, the roles and expectations of a library program were far different from the modern view (Latrobe 1998).

With this limited exposure to model school library programs, today's school leaders, teachers, and higher education faculty must base their views of school library programs upon their own school experiences or base their views on the prevailing educational literature. Despite numerous studies linking effective school libraries to higher student achievement, this research has not been effectively disseminated in journals written for educational administrators, teachers, and/or higher education faculty. Most of this information has been published to an audience of librarians.

In a ten-year longitudinal study by Holzberlein (1971) the contents of 14 professional school administrator journals from 1960-69 were reviewed. One of the most obvious omissions from the topics covered during these years was research-based literature concerning the school library and its effect on student achievement. Holzberlein concluded by pointing out the need for more library-relevant theory and research in professional education journals. However, a recent sampling of the spring issues of 14 major journals for educational administrators and teachers failed to identify a single article concerning school libraries.

If the past experience of school leaders is based on such a narrow view of the school library and current professional journals ignore the relevance of school library issues, then it becomes incumbent upon higher education faculty to instill within these future school leaders the importance of a quality school library program and the impact it has upon student learning.

A COLLABORATIVE EFFORT TOWARDS CHANGE

Recognizing the value of library media services in the school and its impact on student learning, faculty from the University of Southern Mississippi's (USM) Department of Education Leadership and Research, School of Library and Information Science, and University Libraries joined with librarians from a local public high school to work together toward instituting curricular changes in the school's Principal Preparation Program in order to ensure that pre-service administrators possess the necessary skills to supervise and support quality library media programs.

The endeavor began by recognizing the need graduate students have in regards to personal information literacy, which led to a combined effort between faculty in the Department of Educational Leadership and Research and the University Libraries to plan and conduct information literacy workshops. From these efforts, a dialogue began about the need for these future principals to have a clear understanding of the value of library media services in the school and how to effectively supervise and support such programs. After a few initial meetings, faculty from Library and Information Sciences were included to share their knowledge and expertise. Two ideas emerged from our meetings. We outlined some immediate additions to be made to the educational administration courses being taught. Further, we thought it necessary to gather some additional data about the present function of the state's public school media programs and the perceptions of principals, teachers, and media professional towards the role of their school media program.

IMMEDIATE CHANGES MADE TO COURSEWORK

Prior to these meetings, the Principal Preparation Program at USM had undergone a major reform effort that resulted in a total revision of the existing Master's degree program in Educational Leadership and Research. Traditional 3-hour lecture format courses were revised and integrated into three blocks of thematic instruction. The format shifted from individual coursework taken at will to a team-taught, cohort design that focused on problems-based and field-based learning. Therefore, the addition of library media curricula fit naturally into the sequence of the overall program.

Block I–Landscape of Leadership

This block assists students in understanding the theoretical dimensions of leadership, organizational theory, systems thinking, and understanding who they are as an individual and as a future leader. Key concepts of the block include leadership theory, organizational oversight, self-understanding, educational philosophy, and research consumerism.

The team decided that in addition to the information literacy workshops that students were currently participating in, there needed to be additional readings selected to create an awareness of the value of effective library media programming. Also, it was noted that the current data collection assignment students completed to analyze their current school and district needed to include information related to library media services. The selection of appropriate readings and modifications to the data survey assignment are currently in progress.

Block II—The Principal as Instructional Leader

The second block builds on the concepts presented in Block I as students are progressively challenged to think as an administrator. Students are presented with the idea that principals serve as the instructional leader of the school and must therefore have a clear understanding of issues involving curriculum, instruction, and supervision. Key topics of this block include: improving teaching and learning; curriculum products, process and issues; professional development; targeting student success through measurement and evaluation and action research.

The team recognized an opportunity to present students with the idea that the library media center is a valuable resource for instruction. Library Science faculty created a PowerPoint presentation to highlight key components of an effective library media program, selected appropriate reading materials, and volunteered to serve as guest presenters (along with local school librarians) on the subjects of literacy and collaboration. Faculty members also assisted in the development of a model job description, a model evaluation instrument, and identification of appropriate interview questions for the library media specialist.

Block III—The Principal as Manager

The last block in the Principal Preparation program focuses on the managerial aspects of the principalship. This block serves to synthesize the two previous blocks and the field experiences. Central concepts include leadership accountability; human, fiscal and material resource management; school improvement; school law; and educational equity.

Recognizing that both human and fiscal resources must support effective library media programs, this block was the logical place to discuss budgeting for library media services and facility management issues. Again, appropriate readings were selected and library faculty and local school librarians agreed to serve as guest experts.

ON-GOING CURRICULUM DEVELOPMENT

To gain a better understanding of how school libraries were functioning in the state of Mississippi and to gather supporting evidence of how perceptions shaped that use, a 2-phase survey project was developed. The first survey (completed in Fall 2002) examined school library media programs based on Keith Lance's "Colorado Studies." Information gleaned from the surveys compared practices associated with libraries in schools with high and low academic performances. The results from both phases of this study will guide on-going curricular development efforts and will lead to further identification of quality practices in school library programs in Mississippi. This data, along with research from other states, will be included in administrative preparation coursework to help students understand the role and value of specific qualities of a library program in terms of its contribution to higher academic achievement.

THE SURVEY OF SCHOOL MEDIA PROGRAMS: PHASE ONE

Instrumentation: Lance's work in the field of school library research has provided fellow researchers with a model survey instrument for use in similar studies. Lance's original survey instrument has been modified for several studies in several states, including the present study of school libraries in Mississippi (Lance et al. 1999; Lance, Rodney and Hamilton-Pennell 2000a, 2000b; Smith 2001). The Mississippi instrument is most like the version used in the Texas study (Smith 2001) and was modified to include items specific to the Mississippi educational system. The survey solicited information in the following areas: Demographic Information, Library Management, Library Staff (i.e., number and qualification of staff), Service Hours, Staff Activities, Library Use (i.e., use of library in a typical week, library schedule, use by teachers), Technology, Collections and Budget. (A copy of the instrument is available at: http://ocean.otr.usm.edu/~mapplin/MSSurvey.doc.)

Method: A list of potential participants for this study was provided by the Mississippi State Department of Education. In the spring of 2002 a survey was mailed to the librarian of every public school in the Mississippi. Each librarian was asked to complete a survey and return it in the provided, self-addressed, stamped envelope.

The response rate from the original 834 librarians contacted was 19% and included 149 surveys from librarians from schools whose districts were classified as *successful* and 11 surveys from librarians from schools whose districts were classified as *unsuccessful* (see *Assigned Performance Ratings* section below). Follow-up phone calls were made to schools in low-performing school districts in order to increase the representation from these schools. However, the return rate among unsuccessful schools was very low. It is intuitively plausible that librarians in lower performing schools had less time, staff, librarian involvement, and/or accurate accounting systems that would have facilitated the return of completed surveys. In fact, we found during follow-ups with lower performing schools that few, if any, had phones in the library. Also, it was common during a follow-up conversation to learn that many of these librarians actually were serving more than one school site and/or were in their first year in the library and had little knowledge of the information being asked for in the survey.

Assigned Performance Ratings: At the time surveys were distributed, the school accreditation system in the state of Mississippi was undergoing substantial revision. Until the revised system could be implemented, The Mississippi State Department of Education (2002a) chose to freeze all school district accreditation levels as they were assigned in March 1999. Although the revised accreditation model includes school-level accreditation ratings, as opposed to district-level ratings, the new school-level accreditation ratings were not available at the time of this writing. Therefore, only district level accreditation ratings were used in the analyses reported below.

School districts were classified as either *successful* or *unsuccessful* based on the district's assigned accreditation level. Mississippi school district accreditation levels are designated as: Accredited-5-Excellent, Accredited-4-Advanced, Accredited-3-Successful, Accredited-2-Warned, and Accredited-1-Probation (Mississippi State Department of Education 2000). Criteria used in the accreditation model include compliance with general process standards and student performance on standardized tests. For this study, a school was classified as *successful* if it was in a district with an accreditation rating of 3, 4, or 5. A school was classified as *unsuccessful* if it was in a district with an accreditation rating of 1 or 2. Of the 147 school districts and three agricultural high school districts rated by the Mississippi Commission on School Accreditation, 119 districts (79.4%) had accreditation levels of 3, 4, or 5, and 31 districts (20.6%) had accreditation levels of 1 or 2.

Results: Once schools were classified by district accreditation rating, *t-tests* were used to compare the means of the two groups for several items in the survey. Due to a low return rate from *unsuccessful* schools and due to missing data, several items had too few responses for any reasonable comparison. However, in nearly every category, schools classified as *successful* had higher means than those identified as *unsuccessful* (see Table 1). The most notable differences between libraries in successful versus unsuccessful schools can be categorized into five main areas: collections, budget, library use, technology, and staffing. The successful schools in the present sample had more print volumes, more magazine subscriptions, more electronic subscriptions, more video materials, more reference titles on CD-ROM, and more student software packages available for student use. In 2002, libraries in samples of successful schools were allocated 43% more money (M = $8,994.10) than was allocated for library expenditures in the unsuccessful schools (M = $6,274.57). Total expenditures for books averaged $7,605 for successful schools and $6,139 for unsuccessful schools.

In the area of technology, the successful schools had more than twice the number of computers in their libraries; 14 compared to 5.27. Among the successful schools, more than twice as many computers as opposed to the unsuccessful schools were Internet connected or connected to a printer. The implication is that in successful schools students have greater access to electronic research tools in their school library than students in unsuccessful schools.

Additionally, the results indicated that the way libraries were used differed between successful and unsuccessful schools. Successful schools schedule more class time in the library, spend more time allowing students to check out materials, have more individual student research hours, offer more time for reading incentive programs like Accelerated Reader, are used more by faculty members for professional growth and classroom support, and are open more hours beyond the school day. Although libraries in unsuccessful schools report being open more hours during the school day proper, these libraries did not report more student or faculty use during the school day.

Finally, differences in library staff were noted. Successful schools reported that librarians spend more time meeting with the principal, serving on committees, co-teaching lessons with teachers, leading staff development, and providing reading incentives.

Categorization of Schools by Test Data

Results from select standardized tests conducted in the state of Mississippi were analyzed. These included the Mississippi Curriculum Test for Reading in grades two (MCT-R-2), four (MCT-R-4) and eight

TABLE 1. Comparison of Means of Select Characteristics of Libraries in Successful and Unsuccessful Schools as Determined by District Accreditation Level

	Unsuccessful			Successful		
	n	mean	std dev	n	mean	std dev
Collections						
Print Volumes	7	7095.86	6455.1	136	8426.84	4361.11
Magazine Subscriptions	10	19.5	14.04	141	23.05	14.67
Electronic Subscriptions	6	0.17	0.41	125	12.86	134.12
Newspaper Subscriptions	10	2.1	1.37	141	2.02	1.25
Video Materials	9	196.33	127.68	132	399.08	350.94
Reference titles on CD-ROM	9	2.89	2.2	136	10.94	41.78
Student Software Pkgs	7	5.86	7.31	123	14.88	31.71
Budget						
Expenditures–books (sch)	10	4111.35	3125.91	121	4089.65	3510.5
Expenditures–books (other)	5	2027.57	3401.92	72	3515.75	5508.11
Total Operating Budget	9	6274.43	3973.58	120	8994.1	7557.64
Library Use						
Scheduled class time	10	308.9	296.68	141	411.58	309.97
Checking out materials	10	38.9	36.58	137	55.99	94.76
Individual student research	9	169	314.55	129	238.9	289.43
Reading Programs (AR)	8	21.86	19.63	112	49.28	93.02
Faculty–classroom support	11	7.18	6.66	148	17.35	15.14
Faculty–Individual research	10	2.7	3.06	137	4.17	5.8
Faculty–consults w/librarian	10	4.65	7.33	144	8.27	9.63
Faculty–input on acquisitions	10	2.45	3.06	147	4.31	6.08
Hrs open–during school	10	36.65	4.14	149	33.08	10.63
Hrs open–before school	10	1.85	1.99	130	1.98	2.45
Hrs open–after school	10	0.9	1.07	127	2.19	2.91
Hrs open–summer	8	1.88	5.3	136	2.06	10.11
Technology						
Comps in Library–working	11	5.27	2.25	147	14	42.08
Comps in Library–Internet	11	4.12	2.32	147	10.16	14.18
Comps in Library–printers	11	4.73	2.37	146	10.35	14.61
Staff						
Master's or above w/lib cert	8	1	0	88	1.02	0.3
Plans w/teachers	8	2.75	3.06	138	2.28	2.57
Meets w/admin	9	0.83	0.61	131	2.11	3.91
Teaches lesson w/teachers	7	3.57	3.6	129	4.33	6.69
Leads staff development	8	2.38	3.34	135	2.77	7.31
Provides reading incentives	9	3.67	2.87	140	9.29	16.76
Committee work	8	2.13	1.89	134	3.59	5.45

(MCT-R-8), and the Mississippi Subject Area Testing Program English II Test of Reading and Language Conventions (MSATP-ENGII-RLC), administered to tenth-grade students. The use of reading scores as an adequate measure of schools' academic performance was addressed and justified by Lance (1994).

Test scores from these particular grade levels were chosen for three reasons. First, the present sample included elementary, middle and high schools as well as schools that serve combinations of primary, middle and secondary grades, e.g., kindergarten through eighth, kindergarten through twelfth or a combination of middle and high-school grades. Second, test-score information for all schools originally surveyed was not available. Finally, the number of missing responses to several questionnaire items necessitated an approach that would maximize the number of valid responses available for comparisons. In other words, by focusing on these particular grades, we were best able to observe differences between school libraries across a relatively broad range of public schools and do so with the greatest generalizability the data could afford.

Following the precedent set by Rodney, Lance and Hamilton-Pennell (2002) we used *t-tests* to assess differences between the library-related characteristics of low performing schools and the library-related characteristics of high-performing schools at each grade level of interest. In order to differentiate between high and low performing schools at each grade level, median splits were used.

The performance of students in each school was reported by the Mississippi Department of Education as the percentage of students exhibiting "basic" competence on the MCT-R and as students' average score on the SATP ENGII RLC. In the present sample the median percentage of second grade students scoring at the "basic" level was 94.0% (n = 66). Schools in which more than 94.0% of second-graders exhibited "basic" competence in reading were categorized as high-performing schools, whereas schools in which 94.0% or fewer second-graders demonstrated "basic" competence in reading were categorized as low-performing. School performance was similarly categorized as either high or low performing by using sample medians from the MCTR-4 (*Median* = 92.5%, n = 64), the MCTR-8 (*Median* = 78.0%, n = 43), and the SATP ENGII-RLC (*Median* = 303.70, n = 40).

Selection of Dependent Variables

By controlling for several covariates that were not directly related to school libraries, Lance (1994) demonstrated that several factors directly related to school libraries accounted for a significant portion of students' academic performance. Among these library-related effects were the numbers of print volumes, number of electronic subscriptions, expenditures on books, total operating expenses, computer technology in the library and factors related to library staffing.

In the present investigation, a variety of similar information was collected through the mail-out survey and included, (1) total school expenditure per pupil, (2) number of print volumes, (3) electronic subscriptions, (4) total library operating expenses, (5) the number of working computers in the library, (6) the number of computers in the school connected to the Internet, (7) the number of computers in the library with printing available, (8) the number of paid library staff, and (9) the number of library person-hours per week.

Table 2 depicts the results of these tests for the primary schools (grades 2 and 4) in the present sample. Table 3 depicts similar results for the secondary schools. Note that within the present sample and across all four tests, schools in which students scored at or below the median on the relevant standardized tests tend to spend more money per pupil than the schools that reported standardized tests scored above the median. This data supports that of Lance (1994), who found a positive relationship between student test scores and the quality of school libraries and that this relationship was *not* a function of per pupil expenditure. Therefore, the remainder of the findings shown in Table 2 and Table 3 indicate that, within this sample, libraries which are better funded, equipped, and staffed tend to exist in schools with higher academic achievement and that this greater achievement is not a function of more expenditure per pupil.

Although there are few statistically significant differences between libraries from schools with higher standardized test scores, both the significant and the non-significant differences suggest a pattern across all of the schools represented in the sample. This lack of statistical significance was noted in other studies and is explained by Rodney, Lance and Hamilton-Pennell (2002) in this way:

> Statistical significance is an often-misunderstood concept. Usually, when a statistical finding is reported, the first question someone asks is "Is that figure significant?" In this context, the intuitive response is to question the magnitude or size of the figure or the difference between two figures. There are no statistical tests to determine if a difference between two groups is "big enough," particularly if the groups in question represent an entire universe of subjects rather than a sample.

TABLE 2

| | MCT Basic Reading Grade 2 | | | | | | | MCT Basic Reading Grade 4 | | | | | | |
| | High Scoring Schools | | | Low Scoring Schools | | | | High Scoring Schools | | | Low Scoring Schools | | | |
	n	M	SD	n	M	SD	t	n	M	SD	n	M	SD	t
Total school expenditure per pupil	33	5490.1	522.9	29	5852.1	548.7	2.66*	30	5563.5	476.5	30	5812.8	614.6	1.76†
Print Volumes	33	7908.0	3045.2	24	7031.0	4440.3	-0.89	31	7048.0	3259.0	26	8623.0	4588.1	1.51
Electronic Subscriptions	27	0.41	0.75	22	0.23	0.43	-1.00	25	60.28	299.94	24	0.29	0.46	-0.98
TOTAL Library Operating Expenses	30	8681.2	7349.8	23	6965.9	4261.9	-1.00	27	6677.1	5218.4	24	8958.5	6272.5	1.42
# Working Computers in Library	35	21.77	85.08	31	7.84	5.50	-0.91	32	23.88	88.87	32	7.31	4.55	-1.05
# Computers in School Connected to Internet	35	5.69	3.95	31	11.29	25.45	1.29	32	11.06	24.79	32	6.69	5.38	-0.98
# Computers in Library can Print	35	6.43	4.82	31	11.77	26.46	1.17	32	11.03	24.96	32	5.97	4.82	-1.13
# Paid Library Staff	25	1.48	0.51	22	1.41	0.59	-0.44	24	1.42	0.65	26	1.58	0.50	0.98
Library Staff Person–Hours/Week	17	50.9	23.8	14	47.0	22.6	-0.46	18	51.4	20.8	15	57.3	21.2	0.80

Note: High-scoring schools above the sample median on the relevant Mississippi Competence Test (MCT), *$p < .05$, †$p < .10$.

TABLE 3

| | MCT Basic Reading Grade 8 | | | | | | | SATP English RLC | | | | | | |
| | High Scoring Schools | | | Low Scoring Schools | | | | High Scoring Schools | | | Low Scoring Schools | | | |
	n	M	SD	n	M	SD	t	n	M	SD	n	M	SD	t
Total school expenditure per pupil	21	5395.8	563.5	18	5687.8	634.1	1.52	19	5645.4	764.9	19	5799.9	763.1	0.62
Print Volumes	19	8889.6	4162.8	18	6032.3	3551.1	−2.24*	19	10236.0	5579.5	18	9546.5	5425.5	−0.38
Electronic Subscriptions	21	1.52	3.67	17	0.65	0.86	−0.96	18	1.61	2.57	16	0.38	0.72	−1.86†
TOTAL Library Operating Expenses	19	9383.1	7203.2	16	6638.8	3615.9	−1.38	17	12569.4	7387.4	15	5523.9	3892.2	−3.31**
# Working Computers in Library	22	10.27	7.80	20	8.05	4.54	−1.11	20	14.75	13.33	19	13.37	9.73	−0.37
# Computers in School Connected to Internet	22	9.09	8.23	20	7.05	4.30	−0.99	20	13.05	13.89	19	11.63	10.10	−0.36
# Computers in Library can Print	21	9.52	8.33	20	6.90	4.91	−1.22	20	13.45	14.01	19	10.32	9.41	−0.82
# Paid Library Staff	13	1.62	0.65	16	1.31	0.48	−1.44	17	2.03	1.04	15	1.33	0.49	−2.37*
Library Staff Person–Hours/Week	6	57.5	23.0	12	46.2	14.5	−1.29	10	69.8	24.9	8	48.6	17.7	−2.03†

Note: MCT–Mississippi Competence Test, SATP English RLC–SAT Practice test in English Reading and Language Comprehension, **$p < .01$, *$p < .05$, †$p < .10$.

For instance, across all four grade levels the average expenditure per pupil was higher for low-performing schools in this sample than the higher-performing schools. Within the present sample the higher performing schools in grades 2, 8 and 10 reported having more print volumes, more staff hours per week, and higher overall library budgets than the lower performing schools. Across all grade levels, the libraries in the higher-performing schools reported having more computer resources; e.g., computers, print capability, and Internet access; than the lower-performing schools. The conclusion to be drawn is that, within the present sample, students in schools that invest more of their per-pupil expenditure in library-related resources tend to perform better on standardized tests at several grade levels.

SURVEY OF PERCEPTIONS REGARDING SCHOOL LIBRARY PROGRAMS: PHASE II

The second phase of the research project (scheduled for Spring 2003) will include a survey of teachers, principals, and librarians from schools at each state accreditation level. Teachers will be sampled from three groups, beginning, mid-career, and veteran and comparisons will be made. This study will evaluate the perceptions of teachers, librarians and administrators relative to their understanding of the role of school library program and the library professional and how this perception influences the function and ultimately the use and support of the library program in their school. It is hoped that the results of this phase will provide additional supporting evidence for the inclusion of library and information literacy training, not only in the pre-service educational administration programs, but also in programs that prepare teachers as well.

CONCLUSION

The pattern of results in the Mississippi survey of public school libraries is clear: students in schools with better funded, better equipped and better staffed libraries tend to perform better on standardized tests. Although a body of research exists to support this assertion, a void is present in the knowledge possessed by pre-service principals. It is likely that pre-service principals have no effective prior experience to draw from and since current administrator literature is void of information, the need for training in educational administration programs is imperative. Pre-service principal preparation programs must prepare future principals to make wise decisions concerning the support and management of their school's library program and to understand that the library is a vital and essential element in their school's overall educational program.

Though educational administration preparation programs may differ, the information needed by pre-service principals concerning school libraries is essentially the same and can be applied in the course work where appropriate. The primary ideas are:

1. Students in educational administration must themselves be information literate. EDAD faculty can work collaboratively with their academic librarians to ensure that pre-service principals are taught the tenets of information literacy and how it contributes to life-long learning for themselves and for the students they will be serving.

2. Students should be exposed to the research correlating quality library programs with higher student academic achievement. This information should include a discussion about the specific aspects of quality programs that have been demonstrated to positively effect change.

3. Students should learn how to provide appropriate organizational oversight for library programs including budgeting; hiring, evaluating and supervising library staff; facility and technology planning; and how to ensure collaborative planning among all educational partners, e.g., teachers, librarians, administrators. This should be taught in the context of what constitutes a 'quality' school library program.

The groundwork has been laid for departments of educational administration to begin upgrading their curriculums to reflect changes in the role of school library media programs and their effectiveness. These efforts can best be realized through collaborative efforts between those who teach in educational administration preparation programs and academic librarians, local school districts with strong library programs, and other faculty from universities that have implemented successful curricular changes.

REFERENCES

AASL/AECT. 1998. *Information Power: Building Partnerships for Learning.* Chicago: American Library Association.

American Library and Book Trade Annual. 1960. New York: Bowker.

Anthes, Katy. 2002. *"Nobody Wants This Job!" Highlights from the National Forum on Education Policy, 2002.* [online]. [cited 16 February, 2003]. Available from World Wide Web: <http://www.ecs.org/html/meetingsEvents/NF2002/Highlights.asp?recID=6>.

Baughman, James C. 2000. *School Libraries and MCAS Scores.* Boston: Paper presented at a Symposium Sponsored by the Graduate School of Library and Information Science, Simmons College. [cited 10 December, 2002]. Available from World Wide Web: <http://web.simmons.edu/~baughman/mcas-school-libraries/Baughman%20Paper.pdf>.

Cahalan, Margaret. 1987. *Statistics of Public and Private School Library Media Centers, 1985-86: (With Historical Comparisons from 1958-85).* Washington, DC: Center for Education Statistics.

Charter, J. B. 1982. *Case Study Profiles of Six Exemplary Public High School Library Media Programs.* Ph.D. diss., Florida State University.

Coeyman, Marjorie. 2002. *Kids Check Out Refurbished Library.* [online]. Christian Science Monitor [cited 10 January, 2003]. Available from World Wide Web: <http://www.csmonitor.com/2002/0625/p11s01-lepr.html>.

Conners, Maureen. 1984. *The Superintendent's Perception of the School Library Media Center.* Ph.D. diss., Boston University.

Hartzell, Gary. 2002. *What's It Take.* [online]. Institute of Museum and Library Services, White House Conference on School Libraries [cited 17 December, 2002]. Available from World Wide Web: <http://www.imls.gov/pubs/whitehouse0602/garyhartzell.htm>.

Hartzell, Gary. 2002. *Why Should Principals Support School Libraries?* [online]. ERIC Clearinghouse on Information and Technology [cited 17 December, 2002]. Available from World Wide Web: <http://www.ericit.org/digests/EDO-IR-2002-06.shtml>.

Haycock, Ken. 1999. Fostering collaboration, leadership, and information literacy: Common behaviors of uncommon principals and faculties. *NASSP Bulletin*, 83(605): 82-87.

Hellene, D. L. 1973. *The Relationship of Behaviors of Principals in the State of Washington to the Development of School Library Media Programs.* Ph.D. diss., University of Washington.

Holzberlein, Deanne B. 1971. *The Contribution of School Media Programs to Elementary and Secondary Education as Portrayed in Professional Journals Available to School Administrators from 1960-1969.* Ph.D. diss., University of Michigan.

Lance, Keith Curry. 1994. The impact of school library media centers on academic achievement. *School Library Media Quarterly* 22: 167-170+.

Lance, Keith Curry et al. 1999. *Information Empowered: The School Librarian as an Agent of Academic Achievement in Alaska Schools.* [online]. Juneau: Alaska State Library [cited 10 December, 2002]. Available from World Wide Web: <http://www.library.state.ak.us/dev/infoemp.html>.

Lance, Keith Curry, Marcia J. Rodney and Christine Hamilton-Pennell. 2000a. *Measuring Up to Standards: The Impact of School Libraries & Information Literacy in Pennsylvania Schools.* [online]. Greensburg, Pa.: Pennsylvania Citizens for Better Libraries [cited 10 December, 2002]. Available from World Wide Web: <http://www.statelibrary.state.pa.us/libraries/lib/libraries/measuringup.pdf>.

Lance, Keith Curry, Marcia J. Rodney and Christine Hamilton-Pennell. 2000b. *How School Librarians Help Kids Achieve Standards.* [online]. Denver: Library Research Service [cited 10 December, 2002]. Available from World Wide Web: <http://www.lrs.org/documents/lmcstudies/CO/execsumm.pdf>.

Latrobe, Kathy Howard, ed. 1998. *Emerging School Library Media Center: Historical Issues and Perspectives.* Englewood, CO: Libraries Unlimited.

Mississippi State Department of Education. 2000. *Annual Report of the State Superintendent of Education.* [online]. Available from World Wide Web: <http://www.mde. k12.ms.us/account/2000report/Accred99.htm>.

Mississippi State Department of Education. 2002a. *Annual Report of the State Superintendent of Education.* [online]. Available form World Wide Web: <http://www. mde.k12.ms.us/account/2002report/Accred02.htm>.

National Association of Elementary School Principals. *Is There a Shortage of Qualified Candidates for Openings in the Principalship: An Exploratory Study.* [online]. *NAESP Principal Online* [cited 20 December, 2002]. Available from World Wide Web: <http://www.naesp.org/misc/shortage.htm>.

National Center for Education Statistics. 2001. *Post-Secondary Education: Table 232.* [online]. *Digest of Education Statistics.* [cited 17 February, 2003]. Available from World Wide Web: <http://nces.ed.gov/pubs2002/digest2001/tables/dt232.asp>.

Oberg, Dianne, Lyn Hay, and James Henri. 1999. "The Role of the Principal in an Information Literate School Community: Findings from an International Research Project." In L. Lighthall and E. Howe (Eds.), *Unleash the Power! Knowledge, Technology, Diversity: Papers Presented at the Third International Forum on Research in School Librarian,* Seattle, WA: IASL.

Rodney, Marcia J., Keith Curry Lance, and Christine Hamilton-Pennell. 2002. *Make the Connection: Quality School Library Media Programs Impact Academic Achievement in Iowa.* [online]. Bettendorf, Iowa: Mississippi Bend Area Education Agency. [cited 10 December, 2002]. Available from World Wide Web: <http://www.aea9.k12.ia. us/aea_statewide_study.pdf>.

Smith, Ester G. 2001. *Texas School Libraries: Standards, Resources, Services, and Students' Performance.* [online]. Austin, TX: Texas State Library and Archives Commission. [cited 10 December, 2002]. Available from World Wide Web: <http://www. tsl.state.tx.us/ld/pubs/schlibsurvey/>.

United States Office of Education, Library Services Branch. 1965. *National Inventory of Library Needs.* Chicago: American Library Association.

Washington Post. *Slump Is Still Taking Toll on State Budgets; Governors, Lawmakers Make Tough Cuts.* [Lexis-Nexis Academic Universe database online]. Final Edition: A12. [cited 15 December, 2002]. Available from World Wide Web: <http://web. lexis-nexis.com>.

Wilson, Patricia P., and Josette A. Lynders. 2001. *Leadership for Today's School Library: A Handbook for the Library Media Specialist and the School Principal.* Westport, CT: Greenwood Press.

Wright, Whllis E., ed. 1960. *American Library and Book Trade Annual.* New York: Bowker.

Information Literacy Integration in a Doctoral Program

Maria Grant
Marlowe Berg

SUMMARY. Information literacy is critical to those preparing to work as leaders in the realm of education. This study looked at the infusion of information literacy into a new doctoral program, the SDSU-USD Joint Doctoral Program. The ACRL standards were used as a founding point from which to appraise the acquisition of information literacy. Data collection involved faculty review of classes taught within the program as related to the standards. In addition, data regarding the specific methods by which standards were put into effect within the courses were gathered from a focus group comprised of doctoral students currently involved in the program. A means by which to incorporate and verify the inclusion of information literacy standards into the curriculum was developed in the course of this research. Furthermore, exemplars that may serve as models for information literacy inclusion have been established. Of greatest importance, a heightened awareness of the concept of information literacy was manifest in the conversations that occurred between faculty and students. *[Article copies available for a fee from The Haworth Document Delivery Service: 1-800-HAWORTH. E-mail address: <docdelivery@haworthpress.com> Website: <http://www.HaworthPress.com> © 2003 by The Haworth Press, Inc. All rights reserved.]*

Maria Grant is a doctoral student in the San Diego State University/University of San Diego Joint Doctoral Program, College of Education, San Diego State University, San Diego, CA (E-mail: mgrant01@san.rr.com).

Marlowe Berg is Director of the Doctorate in Education Program, San Diego State University and University of San Diego, College of Education, San Diego State University, San Diego, CA (E-mail: berg@mail.sdsu.edu).

[Haworth co-indexing entry note]: "Information Literacy Integration in a Doctoral Program." Grant, Maria, and Marlowe Berg. Co-published simultaneously in *Behavioral & Social Sciences Librarian* (The Haworth Information Press, an imprint of The Haworth Press, Inc.) Vol. 22, No. 1, 2003, pp. 115-128; and: *Information Literacy Instruction for Educators: Professional Knowledge for an Information Age* (ed: Dawn M. Shinew, and Scott Walter) The Haworth Information Press, an imprint of The Haworth Press, Inc., 2003, pp. 115-128. Single or multiple copies of this article are available for a fee from The Haworth Document Delivery Service [1-800-HAWORTH, 9:00 a.m. - 5:00 p.m. (EST). E-mail address: docdelivery@haworthpress.com].

Digital Object Identifier: 10.1300/J103v22n01_08

KEYWORDS. Information literacy, doctoral education, ACRL standards, education programs, COLD grant program

Information literacy is a foundational pillar of research and scholarship. In this age of information proliferation, it becomes an even more critical skill as scholars work to access and evaluate the myriad of information sources available. While critical in academic settings, information literacy extends into all aspects of 21st century life where information and its productive and ethical use lie at the heart of global interactions.

A significant aspect of information literacy is found where information and technology intersect. Schlechty (1996) has long asserted that we labor in an information age serviced by technologies, and the product of this work is knowledge. He goes on to say that an individual's most significant skill in developing knowledge is the ability to work critically with data drawn from a variety of sources through a mixture of mediated forms.

Reinking et al. (1998) argue that "we are heading toward a post-typographic world; that is, one in which printed texts are no longer dominant" (ix). They note that, while it might seem ironic that their message is carried in the form of a conventional textbook, the technological underpinnings of the text, including frequent e-mail messages among the editors and authors, extensive research conducted in multiple media formats, and decisions about which portions of the text would be made available on the World Wide Web, are woven throughout the thinking, writing, and final production of the publication.

In her 1984 dissertation, Alire conducted a nationwide survey of doctoral students regarding library knowledge and resources. Over two-thirds of the students surveyed indicated that knowledge of the library and related resources was significant to their success. More than one half of the students reported that they felt deficient in their library knowledge. In addition, most students stated that they would sign up for a course in library research methodology if it were an option.

Morner (1995) used a test of library research skills to look at doctoral students in an education program as a part of her dissertation. Subjects included 149 students at three private universities in Massachusetts. Morner concluded that the knowledge of library skills possessed by graduate students is limited. Such students are in great need of skills augmentation in the realm of information literacy if high quality literature reviews and strong research reports are to be generated. Similarly, Murry et al. (1997), in a study at the University of Arkansas, found that graduate students in the College of Education's Higher Education Leadership program possessed library research skills that were either inadequate or nonexistent. According to the researchers, such skills are indispensable for the preparation of papers, presentations, and dissertations. More importantly, graduate students preparing to hold positions of leadership need to be able to locate information in their quest to solve "real world" problems. A guidebook was subsequently developed at the University of Arkansas to assist graduate students in their understanding of information literacy.

According to Grafstein (2002), it is the role of faculty to impart those information literacy skills that are embedded within the research paradigms of their disciplines. Additionally, Orr et al. (2001) point out that, oftentimes, faculty are not aware that information literacy must be taught. They tend to view information literacy as a set of skills to be naturally acquired as the process of learning moves forward. To combat this perspective, a new paradigm must be brought to the forefront–one that acknowledges the responsibility of faculty to consciously promote the skills necessary to become information literate.

The integration of information literacy strategies into graduate programs is of considerable import. Because such studies, especially those focusing on doctoral students, are sparse, more exploration in the form of research is needed.

JOINT DOCTORATE IN EDUCATION

In September 2000, San Diego State University and the University of San Diego inaugurated a Joint Doctorate in Education designed to prepare leaders in the field of educational technology and literacy. The intent of the program is to train leaders in the areas of education where a demand for innovative, creative leadership is anticipated. The launch of this program is a response to the ongoing development of new technologies that will continue to modify the ways in which knowledge may be acquired in learning situations. In addition, the concept of what constitutes literacy is shifting and expanding.

The faculty members of the two universities have worked together to create a program comprised of students who would concentrate in either educational technology or literacy yet meet in courses where content was related to both fields of study. Seven core courses were selected to provide foundational knowledge for students of both groups. *Major Issues in Education* is a course that focuses on leadership in educational and community settings. Students are guided in the exploration of major problems faced by educators today. The course, *Change Theories and Processes in Education*, prompts students to look at modern change theories in the context of constructing and orchestrating transformations in education. *Equity and Ethics for a Diverse Society* is a seminar exploring policies and perspectives related to the complexities of ideals, beliefs, and standards in society. In *Curriculum and Technology*, students are presented with an examination of teaching, learning, collaboration, and assessment technologies designed to enhance human performance and the representation of knowledge. The concept of knowledge and how it is gained and communicated is presented in the seminar, *Communication and Cognition*. Two research courses round out the program: *Advanced Qualitative Research Design* and *Advanced Quantitative Research*. In the former course, students explore the major traditions of qualitative research and are guided to conduct investigations in areas of interest. The latter course provides instruction in the interpretation and understanding of statistical analysis as it correlates to research in education. The future graduates of the SDSU-USD Joint Doctoral Program are being prepared to tackle the challenges of education from perspectives that may well promote transformation and paradigm shifts. In recognition of the changing face of information generation, acquisition, and storage, the SDSU-USD Joint Doctoral Program organizers developed a program that would allow future graduates to seize learning opportunities in an information age. The program aim is to prepare professionals to create learning environments in a rapidly evolving global society. It soon became evident that, with this intent in mind, the acquisition of information literacy was vital to the program.

INFORMATION LITERACY GRANT AND ACRL STANDARDS

Many points of content intersection became evident. This manifestation drove the decision to investigate these points of intersection in relation to information literacy. At the same time the Council of Library Directors (COLD) of the California State University (CSU) system offered grants for groups in various educational contexts to explore information literacy and its place in education. The grant program established several goals for participants. First, the activities must result in a statement of information competence as a required learning outcome for the degree program. Second, assessment must verify that the students have met the information literacy competence being addressed. In addition, an appropriate member of the library faculty must be involved. Finally, learning outcomes must correlate with the Association of College and Research Libraries (ACRL) standards on information literacy for higher education.

There is currently a push to incorporate instruction designed to foster information literacy into university curriculums. The California State University (CSU) system is sensitive to this forward movement. Consequently, great attention is being paid to the development of programs that will provide scaffolding for students as they move towards increased fluency in the realm of information literacy. Support for programs that look at the incorporation of performance standards at all academic levels, including the doctoral level, is strong.

The ACRL standards are as follows: (1) the information literate student determines the nature and extent of the information needed, (2) the information literate student accesses needed information effectively and efficiently, (3) the information literate student evaluates information and its sources critically and incorporates selected information into his or her knowledge base and value system, (4) the information literate student, individually or as a member of a group, uses information effectively to accomplish a specific purpose, and (5) the information literate student understands many of the economic, legal, and social issues surrounding the use of information and accesses and uses information ethically and legally. More on the standards, as well as specific learning outcomes that may be associated with each standard, is available online at <http://www.ala.org/acrl/il/toolkit/index.html>.

INFORMATION LITERACY PROJECT

In the summer of 2001, San Diego State University became involved in the grant program. A pre-planning group, consisting of lead faculty members and Joint Doctoral Program directors from San Diego State University and the University of San Diego, met to organize the implementation of this project. A matrix was developed to assess the integration of ACRL standards into the core courses of the SDSU-USD Joint Doctoral Program (see Figure 1). A plan was then established to study the integration of information literacy into the core courses. The plan involved the distribution of the matrix to participating faculty members along with instruction to determine which ACRL standards were incorporated in the course and to what degree. A reflection retreat was planned for faculty members who taught courses within the doctoral

FIGURE 1. Matrix of the Association of College and Research Libraries Information Literacy Competency Standards for Higher Education and the Core Courses for the Program

	Major Issues	Change Theories	Equity and Ethics	Curric and Tech	Commu and Cognit	Qualitat Research	Quantit Research
Stand 1							
Stand 2							
Stand 3							
Stand 4							
Stand 5							

program, program directors, and a library faculty representative. In addition to actively participating in the retreat, the library representative offered instruction designed to familiarize students with research tools and information resources available both at the library and through the online system. The purpose of the retreat was to review the levels of standards incorporation into the core courses in light of the instruction already completed.

The foundational intent of this study was first to identify the points of intersection and then to evaluate the level to which these points were integrated into the curriculum of the core courses. Contributions to this project were made by both faculty and students involved in the Joint Doctoral Program. The aim, at the onset of the project, was to ultimately formulate an integrated definition of information literacy competence. This goal was driven by the question–what does information literacy look like at the doctoral level? The objective was to lend clarity and explicitness to the content of the courses as they related to information literacy. In the end, the project evolved into an unexpected conversation regarding the development of the Joint Doctoral Program. Information literacy was clearly brought to the forefront for discussion by stakeholders.

METHODOLOGY

At the center of the study were three major questions: (1) Which of the information literacy standards and competencies are integrated throughout the program and in what ways is the integration taking place? (2) Which competencies are emphasized strongly across courses, and which competencies are basically, yet sufficiently, covered? (3) What evidence do we have, in the form of exemplars offered by constituents of the program, to support the assertions that competencies are emphasized? These questions focused the study at its inception; however, it became clear as the work progressed that the great value of this project would be manifest in the discourse that evolved around the questions.

Preliminary discussions with select faculty were held to review the concept of information literacy, the standards from ACRL, and the sub-set of performances within each standard. Faculty volunteered examples of activities that incorporated information literacy performances, conducted within their courses, to inform the conversation. These exemplars set the stage for individual faculty reflection concerning what actions, related to information literacy, had occurred within the context of their courses.

A review of the literature clearly illuminated the need for both faculty and students to be involved in the integration of information literacy into any new or existing educational program. In September 2001, faculty members of the Joint Doctoral Program received a copy of the matrix. The matrix consisted of a grid whose rows listed the ACRL standards, along with related subcategories, and whose columns were titled with the core courses. Each core course instructor was given the charge of indicating which standards were most prominent in his/her course.

Core course faculty from SDSU and USD met in a retreat setting to review the goals and specifics of the study. Critical elements were identified as being significant based on relevance to information literacy and information technology. The ACRL standards were presented to faculty members participating in the Joint Doctoral Program as a means of identifying instructional objectives and learning outcomes that can be associated with information literacy. Conversations ensued, leading to an understanding of instruction and methodology as related to the incorporation of literacy and educational technology into the doctoral curriculum. In addition, faculty discussed the performances within each standard with the goal of coming to a mutual understanding of meaning. The collective effort culminated in a look at the following: What comprises information literacy? What is an integrated definition of information literacy competence? Finally, which standards were emphasized in the doctoral program and what exemplars best illustrate the emphasized standards? Faculty responses were transcribed onto a master document so that patterns and major concepts could be determined.

Following the retreat, the instructors of the core courses were asked to identify which of the performances within the standards they emphasized, which they covered to an adequate degree, and which they planned to cover but had not yet done. A coding system was used whereby a "1" was used to represent a performance that was strongly emphasized, a "2" represented a performance that was covered adequately, and a "3" indicated that the performance needed to be developed. Faculty agreed that an emphasized performance entailed multiple opportunities for inclusion within the structure of course activities. Adequate coverage was designated by at least one major instance of the performance in the conduct of course activities. Opportunities to check and re-evaluate coding decisions were provided for faculty throughout the project.

A symbol system was implemented whereby a star represented an "emphasized" performance in a course (see Figure 2), and a dot was chosen to represent an "adequately" covered performance in a course (see Figure 3). For example, the performance, "identifies a need for information," was emphasized in five of the core courses. This would be signified by the presence of five stars on the matrix. There was now an understanding that all ACRL standards were being covered. This revelation led to the desire to discern which aspects of the courses were exemplified as elements of information literacy as viewed by the students in the program.

In an attempt to clarify and triangulate this data, a focus group, consisting of four current doctoral students from both the educational technology and the literacy cohorts, was assembled. Focus groups are used extensively in marketing research to gain insights and to produce data through the interaction of participants. According to Gibbs (1997), the main purpose of focus group research is to draw upon respondents' attitudes, feelings, beliefs, experiences, and reactions in a way that would not be achievable with other methods of gathering data. The attitudes and beliefs sought after by researchers are often revealed via the social gathering and interaction that is at the heart of focus groups. Focus group participants were cohort students who expressed an interest in participating as volunteers. The task, as presented to the group, involved the development of descriptions of exemplars from the courses where "emphasized" performances were reported by faculty. A "chain of ideas" activity was used to facilitate the formulation of the descriptors. The chaining strategy allows for multiple reviews of ideas and consensus regarding a description of the experience. A reporting form, which had the "emphasized" performances listed, was developed specifically for this activity. Each of the four students was given the form for one course. In this activity, focus group participants were asked to spend approximately five minutes writing down all class assignments, activities, and/or projects undertaken in a specified core

FIGURE 2. Emphasis Matrices

This figure shows one of the matrices that present a summary of the data across the core courses. Each star signifies that the standard is emphasized in a core course. Standards that are reported to be emphasized in three or more core courses are considered to be highly emphasized aspects of the joint doctoral program. Matrices presenting the summaries for the rest of the ILC Standards are available from the authors upon request.

ILC: STANDARD ONE THE INFORMATION LITERATE STUDENT DETERMINES THE NATURE AND EXTENT OF INFORMATION NEEDED.	
IDENTIFIES A NEED FOR INFORMATION	★ ★ ★ ★ ★
USES CRITERIA TO EVALUATE INFORMATION	★ ★ ★ ★
COMBINES EXISTING INFORMATION WITH NEW IDEAS	★ ★ ★
IDENTIFIES KEY CONCEPTS ASSOCIATED WITH A TOPIC	★ ★ ★
IDENTIFIES VARIOUS SOURCES AND FORMATS OF POTENTIAL INFORMATION	★ ★ ★
USES RAW DATA FROM PRIMARY SOURCES	★ ★ ★
ACCESSES RESOURCES FROM MULTIPLE SOURCES, OFTEN NOT LOCAL.	★ ★ ★

course if they satisfied a specific performance. After the five-minute time period had passed, each form was passed on to another focus group member. As the activity progressed, every group member was given the opportunity to complete all forms for all core courses. As the forms moved through the group, participants were encouraged to comment or expound on the responses or ideas presented by their colleagues. The fast-paced nature of the activity was designed to foster a brainstorm episode. In this manner, a well-rounded, thorough review of the course activities as they related to the standards, was developed. Further analysis of the focus group responses showed that much agreement existed between members. For example, to fulfill the performance that required the conduction of activities that would "demonstrate a need for information," group members reported the following: "The Change course curriculum involved the generation of a Problem Based Learning project based on a selected change theory. The gathering and analysis of information was integral to this assignment" (see Figure 4). The focus group activity served two purposes. First, the obvious goal of establish-

FIGURE 3. Standards Covered Matrices

This figure shows the matrices that present a summary of the data across the core courses. Each dot signifies that the standard is covered in a core course. Standards that are reported to be covered in three or more cores courses are considered to be sufficiently covered aspects of the joint doctoral program. Matrices presenting the summaries for the rest of the ILC Standards are available from the authors upon request.

ILC: STANDARD ONE THE INFORMATION LITERATE STUDENT DETERMINES THE NATURE AND EXTENT OF INFORMATION NEEDED.	
COMBINES EXISTING INFORMATION WITH NEW IDEAS	• • • •
IDENTIFIES VARIOUS SOURCES AND FORMATS OF POTENTIAL INFORMATION	• • • •
IDENTIFIES KEY CONCEPTS ASSOCIATED WITH A TOPIC	• • •

ing exemplars of "emphasized" performances was completed. Second, the more subtle aim of fostering conversations that would generate a conscious awareness of the ACRL standards as they specifically related to the SDSU-USD Joint Doctoral Program, was clearly accomplished.

The methodology used in this study was chosen as a means to tap into the content of the doctoral program as it related to the establishment of information literacy. Methods involved the extraction of data from the program constituents, including faculty and students. In this manner, the research evolved into a self-study and a stimulus for dialogue regarding the significance of information literacy.

ANALYSIS OF DATA

Data collection centered around three significant questions: (1) Which of the information literacy standards and competencies are integrated throughout the program and in what ways is the integration taking place? (2) Which competencies are emphasized strongly across courses, and which competencies are basically, yet sufficiently, covered? (3) What evidence do we have, in the form of exemplars offered by constituents of the program, to support the assertions that competencies are emphasized?

Upon completion of the degree of emphasis task, data were tallied across the matrix. A review of the data showed that all performances were

FIGURE 4. Sample Exemplars

EXAMPLES OF ACTIVITIES THAT EMPHASIZE A NEED FOR INFORMATION

A) The need for information was made clear in the initial weeks of each course in the program. As a specific example, the Qualitative and Quantitative courses may be noted for the inclusion of perspectives concerning the need and composition of a researchable question.
B) The Change course curriculum involved the generation of a Problem Based Learning project based on a selected change theory. The gathering and analysis of information was integral to this assignment.
C) The Quantitative Research course has emphasized the need for information in the form of statistical data gathering that could be used in an analysis program such as SPSS.

EXAMPLES OF ACTIVITIES THAT FOSTER THE USE OF CRITERIA TO EVALUATE INFORMATION

A) Several courses have required literature reviews. The process of composing a literature review has entailed the use of criteria to evaluate information.
B) The Change course curriculum required students to evaluate change theories in the forum of a synthesis paper.
C) In the Quantitative Research course the evaluation of data for validity has been a focus.

EXAMPLES OF ACTIVITIES THAT FOSTER THE USE OF EXISTING INFORMATION ALONG WITH NEW IDEAS

A) Several classes have either required or encouraged the development of a publishable paper. This typically has involved a synthesis of information along with the incorporation of original research.
B) The Major Issues course required a deliverable product in the form of a multi-media presentation. This was the culmination of a compilation of ideas and information.

---

covered in at least three core courses, some to an "adequate" degree and many at the "emphasized" level. Focus group data established that students were able to extract examples of information literacy performances and were in agreement regarding the manifestation of these exemplars.

FINDINGS

The data collected from faculty showed that doctoral students participating in all core courses were engaged in activities related to all five of the ACRL standards. Each of the five standards was emphasized in some capacity.

Emphasis of Performances

The emphasis of Standard One was established in content designed to foster the ability to: identify of a need for information; use criteria to evaluate information; combine existing information with new ideas; identify key concepts associated with a topic; identify various sources of potential information; use raw data from primary sources; and access resources from multiple sources, often not local. Standard Two was emphasized in content created to foster the ability to: retrieve information from online sources and develop a research plan appropriate to a research methodology. Standard Three was emphasized through instruction developed to enable students to: recognize differing viewpoints; make value judgments regarding various viewpoints; understand how to extract relevant information and organize in own words; critically examine resources in terms of validity, reliability and accuracy; construct new hypotheses from existing information; analyze information with the assistance of a computer and other technologies; critically evaluate information; and discuss the efficacy of information with subject experts and practitioners. Standard Four was emphasized in curriculum designed to: enhance the students' capacity to systematically seek, collect, and evaluate information; communicate content of a product to others; use a range of technology to create a product; and organize content to support an appropriate format of a product. Finally, Standard Five was emphasized in the content focusing on the students' acquisition of the ability to: show an understanding of intellectual property, fair use, and copyright and preserve and honor the integrity of information resources including texts, data, images, and sounds.

Performance Coverage

In addition, each of the five standards was covered basically and sufficiently in the following ways. Standard One was covered through content designed to allow students to: combine existing information with new ideas; identify various sources and formats of potential information; and identify key concepts associated with a topic. Standard Two was covered through instruction leading to the capability to understand the syntax of recording various types of sources/citations. Standard Three was covered by curriculum focusing on the ability to: consider the impact of context on the interpretation of information; review and evaluate whether sufficient information-gathering has taken place; effectively quote from source material; critically examine resources for accuracy, validity, and reliability; recognize bias and manipulation; and synthesize information into useful primary statements. Standard Four was covered through curriculum promoting the manipulation of digital text. Finally, Standard Five was covered in content that prompted students to: understand legal, ethical, and socioeconomic issues related to information and information technology; follow appropriate "netiquette" when using electronic communications; use appropriate documentation form when citing resources; become aware of fee-based and free access to information; and understand and comply with institutional regulations related to information resources.

Focus Group Performance Indicators

The data gathered from the student focus group provided evidence, in the form of exemplars, that standards are being emphasized in specific ways. Many of the exemplars described by the doctoral students, who comprised the focus group, were related to the development of projects or professional style papers. For example, several courses provided activities that focused on the use of criteria to evaluate information. The process of composing literature reviews was specifically mentioned as an exemplar for Standard One. In other cases, exemplars related to the content of the course. In the Change Theory class, students were lead through an evaluation of various change theories in the forum of a synthesis paper. Both the Qualitative and Quantitative Research classes presented students with guidelines for critically evaluating data for validity. As is evident in these examples, the curriculum in many courses incorporated the gathering, understanding, and use of information within the context of projects, papers, and presentations. This methodology enabled instructors to cover several standards under one big umbrella. Students were challenged to gain practical experience and knowledge through activities that incorporated the information literacy standards.

CONCLUSION

The attainment of information literacy is a foundational element in the pursuit of research. The SDSU-USD Joint Doctoral Program was developed to provide students with the opportunity to gain the skills and knowledge needed to create and foster the growth of novel and effective learning situations both in the realm of academia and in the private sector. The intersection between educational technology and teaching and learning is found within the exemplars of information literacy. The Information Literacy Grant provided the faculty and student members of the Joint Doctoral Program with the opportunity to develop a model for data collection and for the compilation of collective responses. The creation and organization of the matrices clearly show where and how the core courses are meeting the ACRL standards. They provide a transparent and graphical means by which to understand information literacy integration within a doctoral program. Each exemplar stands as an archetype for those wishing to develop a doctoral program that incorporates an underpinning of information literacy.

In addition, the data collection tasks, accomplished by both faculty and students, served to create a common point of discourse. Faculty members and doctoral students found themselves participating in conversations centered on information literacy. An awareness of information literacy–the meaning, the manifestation in a graduate level course, and the significance to doctoral students–was brought to the conscious level of all stakeholders. Finally, of greatest consequence to the SDSU-USD Joint Doctoral Program, is the reality that meaningful conversations are ongoing.

REFERENCES

Alire, Camilla. A. 1984. *A nationwide survey of education doctoral students' attitudes regarding the importance of the library and the need for bibliographic instruction.* Doctoral dissertation, University of Northern Colorado.

Gibbs, Anita. 1997. *Social research update 19: Focus groups* [online]. Surrey, England: Department of Sociology, University of Surrey [cited 5 February 2003]. Available World Wide Web <http://www.soc.surrey.ac.uk/sru/SRU19.html>.

Grafstein, Ann. 2002. A discipline-based approach to information literacy. *The Journal of Academic Librarianship* 28 (4): 197-204.

Morner, Claudia J. 1993. *A test of library research skills for doctoral students.* Doctoral dissertation. Boston College.

Murry, John W., Jr., Elizabeth C. McKee, and James O. Hammons. 1997. Faculty and librarian collaboration: The road to information literacy for graduate students. *Journal on College Teaching* 8 (2): 107-121.

Orr, Debbie, Margaret Appleton, and Margie Wallin. 2001. Information literacy and flexible delivery: Creating a conceptual framework and model. *The Journal of Academic Librarianship* 27 (6): 457-463.

Reinking, David et al. (Eds.) 1998. *Handbook of literacy and technology: Transformations in a post-typographic World.* Mahwah, NJ: Lawrence Erlbaum.

Schlechty, Phillip. 1996. *Schools for the twenty-first century.* San Francisco, Jossey-Bass.

Information Literacy
in Pre-Service Teacher Education:
An Annotated Bibliography

Corey M. Johnson
Lorena O'English

SUMMARY. This annotated bibliography presents a review of articles published on the topic of information literacy in teacher education since the late 1980s. Many of the articles outline concerns about pre-service teachers who graduate with insufficient information literacy skills, who are unprepared to teach these skills to their future students, and who do not understand the role of the school librarian as an instructional collaborator. On the other hand, many articles describe innovative and successful programs where exposure to librarians, integration of information literacy instruction, attention to library research, or introduction of a process approach to information use can produce new teachers who are equipped to collaborate with school librarians and to teach information literacy skills to their students. *[Article copies available for a fee from The Haworth Document Delivery Service: 1-800-HAWORTH. E-mail address: <docdelivery@haworthpress.com> Website: <http://www.Haworth Press.com> © 2003 by The Haworth Press, Inc. All rights reserved.]*

Corey M. Johnson is Instructional Design Librarian, Washington State University, Pullman, WA (E-mail: coreyj@wsu.edu).

Lorena O'English is Social Sciences Reference and Instruction Librarian, Washington State University, Pullman, WA (E-mail: oenglish@wsu.edu).

[Haworth co-indexing entry note]: "Information Literacy in Pre-Service Teacher Education: An Annotated Bibliography." Johnson, Corey M., and Lorena O'English. Co-published simultaneously in *Behavioral & Social Sciences Librarian* (The Haworth Information Press, an imprint of The Haworth Press, Inc.) Vol. 22, No. 1, 2003, pp. 129-139; and: *Information Literacy Instruction for Educators: Professional Knowledge for an Information Age* (ed: Dawn M. Shinew, and Scott Walter) The Haworth Information Press, an imprint of The Haworth Press, Inc., 2003, pp. 129-139. Single or multiple copies of this article are available for a fee from The Haworth Document Delivery Service [1-800-HAWORTH, 9:00 a.m. - 5:00 p.m. (EST). E-mail address: docdelivery@haworthpress.com].

Digital Object Identifier: 10.1300/J103v22n01_09

KEYWORDS. Information literacy, library instruction, teacher education, annotated bibliography, pre-service teachers, school librarians, media centers

Over the past 15 years, librarians and other educators have consistently written about the relationship between information literacy instruction and teacher education. The need for greater attention to this issue was made clear, for example, in the K-12 information literacy standards, *Information Power: Guidelines for School Library Media Programs* (1988), and has been reiterated in national reports such as the Association of College and Research Libraries' *Progress Report on Information Literacy* (1998), and the *Blueprint for Collaboration* (2000) issued by a joint committee of academic and school librarians.

A review of articles published on the topic of information literacy in teacher education during this time shows a number of common themes in the literature. For example, many writers identify a focus in teacher education on the "information access and delivery" role of school librarians over that of "collaborative partner and information literacy specialist." Other authors identify innovative projects and successful programs that demonstrate how a teacher education curriculum that incorporates exposure to librarians, information literacy instruction, and library research, can result in real changes in pre-service teacher attitudes toward working with school librarians. Finally, several authors argue that pre-service teachers who have been exposed to a well-defined and integrated program of information literacy instruction will move into the profession better equipped to engage in significant instructional partnerships with their school librarians and to teach information literacy skills to their students.

While this bibliography represents only a small part of the total body of literature in this area, it reflects a representative sampling of key works. Readers interested in reviewing earlier works in this field are urged to consult the earlier review of the literature found in O'Hanlon (1988), on which this collection builds.

* * *

ACRL Education and Behavioral Sciences Section. 1992. "Information Retrieval and Evaluation Skills for Education Students." *College and Research Libraries News* 53: 583-588.

This document is a revision of the 1981 "Bibliographic competencies for education students" and presents a comprehensive listing of what education students need to know about libraries and information literacy. These guidelines reflect initiatives that emphasize critical thinking, problem-solving skills, active learning, and demonstration of skills in seeking, retrieving, and evaluating information. Their purpose is to assist instruction librarians in working with education faculty and aid in the creation of specific learning objectives for library instructional sessions and education coursework. A series of goals, objectives, and sub-objectives are listed in each of five central areas: generation and communication of knowledge in education, intellectual access, bibliographic representation of information sources, physical access and evaluation of information sources, and collaborative roles of teachers and school library media specialists. The article concludes with two lesson plan examples illustrating the basic skills identified in the document.

Asselin, Marlene. 2000. "Poised for Change: Effects of a Teacher Education Project on Pre-Service Teachers' Knowledge of the School Library Program and the Role of the Teacher-Librarian." *School Libraries Worldwide* **6: 72-87.**

Asselin describes the Information Literacy Project of the University of British Columbia (Canada), a program that works with pre-service teachers to make them more aware of the role of the teacher-librarian and of school libraries in integrated and collaborative instructional programs. Students work with teacher-librarians on curriculum design using resource-based learning. Using pre- and post-tests, the study looked at the areas of information literacy, critical thinking and resource-based learning and found an increase in understanding in all three areas, along with an increased awareness of the role of the teacher-librarian. Asselin suggests teacher educators take a leadership role in the development of partnerships such as this.

Asselin, Marlene, and Elizabeth A. Lee. 2002. " 'I Wish Someone Had Taught Me': Information Literacy in a Teacher Education Program." *Teacher Librarian* **30: 10-17.**

Asselin notes that ongoing concerns about lifelong learning and the recent inclusion of information literacy instruction in national education guidelines demonstrate the need for teachers to become information literate as part of their pre-service education. She discusses a Canadian initiative to include information literacy instruction in the literacy education coursework offered to pre-service teachers. This model highlights process-based problem solving, resource-based learning, and collaboration with school librarians with the aim of better preparing pre-service teachers to bring information literacy content into their own teaching.

Callison, Daniel. 1995. "Restructuring Pre-Service Education." In *School Library Media Annual,* **edited by Betty J. Morris, 100-112. Englewood, Colorado: Libraries Unlimited.**

Callison identifies a number of issues that he believes limits pre-service teachers' ability to collaborate effectively with school librarians. Among these are the isolation that pre-service teachers new to a school can experience, and the lack of experience that pre-service teachers have during their professional education with resource-based models of instruction. Callison argues that teacher educators must model resource-based teaching for their students in order to prepare pre-service teachers to collaborate with school librarians on instructional design. He also calls upon school librarians to make a special effort to offer to collaborate with the student teachers in their buildings.

Carr, Jo Ann. 1998. *Information Literacy and Teacher Education.* **(Report No. SP038201). Washington, District of Columbia: ERIC Clearinghouse on Teaching and Teacher Education. (ERIC Document Reproduction Service No. ED424231).**

Carr reports that efforts to incorporate information literacy into the pre-service curriculum have been largely unsuccessful, although standards covering information literacy skills are increasingly being written by professional and accrediting associations. Carr outlines existing models for integrating course-related information literacy instruction into student teacher education. This article provides an excellent overview of the reasons why teachers need to learn about information literacy during their pre-service education and can serve as an effective springboard to collaborative activities on your own campus.

Carr, Jo Ann and Kenneth Zeichner. 1988. "Academic Libraries and Teacher Education Reform: The Education of the Professional Teacher." In *Libraries and the Search for Academic Excellence,* **edited by Patricia Senn Breivik & Robert Wedgeworth, 83-92. London: The Scarecrow Press.**

Addressing educational reform proposals issued during the 1980s, Carr and Zeichner outline three areas that may have an impact on library services for teacher education programs: transforming teacher education from an undergraduate to a graduate program; strengthening the academic and field experience components of teacher education; and, focusing on the professional autonomy of teachers. The authors argue that each of these proposals, if enacted, could transform academic library support for teacher education programs, and urge librarians to be proactive in tailoring materials and services to meet the need of evolving pre-service programs.

D'Amicantonio, John and Jordan M. Scepanski. 1997. "Strengthening Teacher Preparation Through a Library Program." *Education Libraries* **21: 11-16.**

D'Amicantonio and Scepanski note the role that librarians can play in enhancing teacher training programs, and describe activities in place at the library at California State University, Long Beach (CSULB), including: extensive library instruction sessions that emphasize critical thinking, and a proposed partnership with a local high school to link its online catalog to the CSULB catalog in order to provide pre-service teachers with information about materials currently available in high school library collections.

Doiron, Ray. 1999. *University/School Library Collaborations to Integrate Information Technology into Resource-Based Learning Activities.* **(Report No. IR057600). Birmingham, AL: International Association of School Librarianship. (ERIC Document Reproduction Service No. ED437064).**

Doiron and colleagues at the University of Prince Edward Island (Canada) studied the impact of involving pre-service teachers in authentic learning collaborations with school librarians and others to develop information technology projects. Three areas were analyzed: the curriculum process, the use of information technology in teaching, and collaboration with school librarians. In each case, respondents expressed respect for abilities of school librarians while gaining valuable experience in problem solving and instructional collaboration. Doiron suggests that authentic projects like this empower pre-service teachers and make them aware of the instructional support available from school librarians.

Duling, Sandra and Patrick Max. 1995. "Teaching the Teachers in an Electronic Environment." In *Twenty-First National LOEX Library Instruction Conference: The Impact of Technology on Library Instruction*, edited by Linda Shirato, 103-112. Eastern Michigan University: LOEX Clearinghouse.

Max and Duling present two speeches on the impact of educational reform and technological change on the relationship between teachers and librarians. Max argues that technology can support instructional objectives, but it must not be accepted without critical evaluation. Duling discusses the school restructuring movement at the K-12 level and how its goals dovetail with those of the information literacy movement. Duling draws special attention to the emerging information needs of teachers involved in site-based management and how the need for teachers to make use of research literature to solve local problems suggests new directions for the information literacy instruction provided to pre-service teachers.

Franklin, Godfrey and Ronald C. Toifel. 1994. "The Effects of BI on Library Knowledge and Skills Among Education Students." *Research Strategies* 4: 224-237.

Franklin and Toifel outline a 1991 study conducted at the University of West Florida that focused on the effectiveness of information literacy instruction provided for undergraduate (n = 142) and graduate (n = 39) students in education. A pre-test and post-test model was used to assess student learning in three areas: general knowledge about the library, knowledge about using the online catalog, and knowledge about ERIC and other education specific databases. Information literacy instruction was integrated into course assignments requiring use of library resources. The authors found statistically significant improvement in all areas between the pre-test and post-test, although the overall rate of improvement was greater for the undergraduates than for the graduate students.

Gallegos, Bee and Peter Rillero. 1996. "Bibliographic Database Competencies for Pre-Service Teachers." *Journal of Technology and Teacher Education* 4: 231-246.

Gallegos and Rollero argue that searching bibliographic databases for information requires both technology and information literacy. They suggest that the best time for teachers to learn information-seeking skills is during their pre-service education, but worry that students are often over-confident in their searching abilities. Using standards developed by a number of professional associations related to technology and information literacy, the authors identify a set of seven bibliographic database competencies that all teachers should have. Partnerships between teacher educators, teaching faculty, technology educators and librarians are necessary to ensure that student teachers are technologically and information literate.

Hartzell, Gary N. 1997. "The Invisible School Librarian." *School Library Journal* **24: 24-29.**

Hartzell identifies a number of reasons why few K-12 teachers or administrators appear to object strenuously to reductions in school library funding. Chief among these is the failure of teacher and administrator education programs to emphasize the teaching role of the school librarian. If not introduced to the idea of the school librarian as instructional collaborator during pre-service education, teachers and administrators are less likely to recognize this role once they enter the schools. Hartzell recommends that school librarians work to influence the training of future classroom teachers and school administrators in order to assure early recognition of the instructional role of the library.

Hartzell, Gary. 2002. "What's It Take?" *Supplement to Teacher Librarian* **30: 81-86.**

In this article directed at school administrators, Hartzell discusses how administrators often have an incomplete picture of the role of the school librarian. He notes that not only does teacher training itself generally not focus on collaborative work, but that administrators are often trained by former school administrators who rarely recognize the school librarian's potential. Discussing pre-service administrator education, Hartzell reports on a survey that suggested 90% of administrator educators saw no role for the principal in facilitating instructional collaboration between teachers and librarians, and argues that discussion of school library issues in administrator education is often limited to potential problems, e.g., censorship.

Jacobson, Frances. 1988. "Teachers and Library Awareness: Using Bibliographic Instruction in Teacher Preparation Programs." *Reference Services Review* **16: 51-55.**

Jacobson argues that only teachers who have learned library research skills during their pre-service education can effectively transmit such skills to their students. She identifies several examples of effective partnerships between academic libraries and teacher education programs, as well as one exemplary program that moves beyond instruction in research skills to introduce pre-service teachers more effectively to school library resources and services.

O'Brien Libutti, Patricia and Bonnie Gratch. 1995. *Teaching Information Retrieval and Evaluation Skills to Education Students and Practitioners: A Casebook of Applications.* **Chicago: American Library Association.**

This book of case studies features twelve articles. Nearly every article was written by an information professional reflecting on a specific teaching experience with education students. Each article includes introductory information about the instructional session request, a copy of the lesson plan, a narrative of the teaching experience, and a reflective component. A common thread throughout the submissions is the idea that librarians and education students alike benefit from purposeful concentration on being "reflective practitioners."

O'Hanlon, Nancy. 1987. "Library Skills, Critical Thinking, and the Teacher-Training Curriculum." *College & Research Libraries* **48: 17-26.**

O'Hanlon reports the results of a survey of elementary-education faculty in teacher-education programs in Ohio. She concludes that faculty overwhelmingly agreed that library and critical thinking skills instruction should be part of teacher education programs and that schoolteachers enrolled in such programs are better prepared to help their students learn these skills. Even so, only 1/3 of responding faculty assigned projects requiring library research, and of this number, most assumed their students already had reasonably good library skills. Over half of the respondents later reported that their assumptions were incorrect. O'Hanlon also concludes that there was no consensus on the questions of who should be teaching library skills in teacher preparation programs and who should be teaching elementary students these same skills.

O'Hanlon, Nancy. 1988. "The Role of Library Research Instruction in Developing Teachers' Problem Solving Skills." *Journal of Teacher Education* **39: 44-49.**

O'Hanlon argues that more attention needs to be paid to instruction in critical thinking as a foundation for information literacy instruction. She suggests that "guided design" is an instructional model that can encompass instruction in critical thinking, information literacy, and problem-solving skills. O'Hanlon concludes that teacher trainees who are exposed to guided design may use this same curricular structure in their own classrooms, thus nurturing better critical thinkers.

O'Hanlon, Nancy. 1988. "Up the Down Staircase: Establishing Library Instruction Programs for Teachers." *Reference Quarterly* **27: 528-34.**

O'Hanlon examines a century of trends and issues related to information literacy instruction for pre-service teachers. Echoing other studies in which she identifies a link between critical thinking skills and information literacy, O'Hanlon concludes that teacher education programs must embrace a process-oriented approach to information literacy instruction to effectively meet the information needs of teachers. This article is especially valuable for its review of the literature.

Pappas, Marjorie and Ann Teppe. 1995. "Preparing the Information Educator for the Future." In *School Library Media Annual,* **edited by Betty J. Morris, 37-44. Englewood, Colorado: Libraries Unlimited.**

Pappas and Tepe describe the role of school librarians as "information educators." They identify three roles for the school librarian: information manager; curriculum consultant and teacher; and manager of the information center. As information manager, the school librarian concentrates on providing access to information and teaching students to effectively navigate oceans of data. As curriculum consultant and teacher, school librarians will insert information literacy into the curriculum by making a real-world laboratory of the school library and enlisting the support of community members in information instruction. As manager of the information center, school librarians provide leadership and support for the use of new instructional and information technology in the school.

Small, Ruth V. 2002. "Collaboration . . ." *Teacher Librarian* **29: 8-11.**

Small argues that teachers can benefit significantly from collaborating with school librarians, but also that such collaborations are often unsuccessful. One possible reason for this situation, she argues, is the difference between pre-service teacher training and school librarian training. Pre-service teacher education stresses collaboration within disciplines or grade levels, but not beyond; library education emphasizes the importance of collaboration in all areas. Possible remedies include outreach by teacher librarians to pre-service education students as well as collaborations between school librarians and teacher education faculty.

Templeton, Lolly, Signia Warner, and Richard Frank. 2001. "A Collaborative Approach to Integrating Technology and Information Literacy in Pre-Service Teacher Education." In Burkett, Ruth S., Michelle Macy, James A. White, and Carine M. Feyten. (Eds.), *Pre-service Teacher Education {SITE 2001 Section}.* **(Report No. IR020890). Orlando, FL: Society for Information Technology & Teacher Education (ERIC Document Reproduction Service No. ED457833).**

Templeton et al. report a study that uses active learning and constructivist methods to educate pre-service teachers about information literacy. A theoretical framework is provided in the context of current learning theory. The study attempted to determine how the information literacy program aided in pre-service education courses, e.g., what key influences of IL were identified by the pre-service teachers, what were the teacher education faculty attitudes towards IL competency? They conclude that the program had been successful in integrating IL objectives into students' practicums and coursework, and resulted in a recognition on the part of education faculty of the importance of information literacy, the need to share instruction with school librarians, and the importance of formal IL instruction in the pre-service program.

Thurman, Glenda R. 1992. "A Survey of Student Teachers' Library Media Skills: A Replication." In *Proceedings of Selected Research and Development Presentations at the Convention of the Association for Educational Communications and Technology and Sponsored by the Research and Theory Division,* **819-824. Washington: U.S. Department of Education.**

Thurman describes a 1991 study that sought to measure pre-service teachers' knowledge of the availability and use of library services and resources.

A survey instrument was developed and comprised of 22 open-ended questions in four subject areas: bibliographic skills, mediagraphic skills, bibliographic/electronic sources, and perceptions of libraries and librarians. Across each of the first three subject areas, students' responses indicated knowledge of only a small subset of available resources. Respondents also demonstrated a limited idea of what librarians can do for them.

Wilson, Kay. 1997. *Information Skills: The Reflections and Perception of Student Teachers and Related Professionals*. (Report No. IR056590). Vancouver, British Colombia, Canada: International Association of School Librarianship. (ERIC Document Reproduction Service No. ED412946).

Wilson studied the information skills of Scottish pre-service teachers, conducting interviews with teacher educators, secondary school teachers, school librarians, and the student teachers themselves. The study results indicated a general ignorance of what "information skills" are, an inability to see information literacy as a process that had a place outside of the job of a teacher, and an inability to see the individual's own lack of information literacy. Wilson also notes that all the groups studied needed not only to improve their information literacy skills, but also needed to reflect on why information literacy skills were important.

Wolcott, Linda, L., Kimberly A. Lawless, and Deborah Hobbs. 1999. *Assessing Pre-Service Teachers' Beliefs About the Role of the Library Media Specialist*. (Report No. IR057601). Birmingham, AL: International Association of School Librarianship. (ERIC Document Reproduction Service No. ED437065).

Wolcott et al. examine the three roles for teacher-librarians outlined in the 1998 revision of *Information Power*–learning and teaching, information access and delivery, and program administration–and evaluates the extent to which pre-service teachers accept those roles. Results indicated that the pre-service teachers emphasized the information access and delivery role significantly over the other two. This suggests that they will not recognize the collaborative and leadership roles of the school librarian. The authors suggest steps that should be taken to lay the groundwork for librarian-classroom teacher partnerships.

Index

SPECIAL 25%-OFF DISCOUNT!

Order a copy of this book with this form or online at:
http://www.haworthpress.com/store/product.asp?sku=5072
Use Sale Code BOF25 in the online bookshop to receive 25% off!

Information Literacy Instruction for Educators
Professional Knowledge for an Information Age

____ in softbound at $22.46 (regularly $29.95) (ISBN: 0-7890-2073-4)
____ in hardbound at $37.46 (regularly $49.95) (ISBN: 0-7890-2072-6)

COST OF BOOKS _____

Outside USA/ Canada/
Mexico: Add 20%. _____

POSTAGE & HANDLING _____

US: $4.00 for first book & $1.50
for each additional book
Outside US: $5.00 for first book
& $2.00 for each additional book.

SUBTOTAL _____

In Canada: add 7% GST. _____

STATE TAX _____

CA, IL, IN, MIN, NY, OH, & SD residents
please add appropriate local sales tax.

FINAL TOTAL _____

If paying in Canadian funds, convert
using the current exchange rate,
UNESCO coupons welcome.

❏ **BILL ME LATER:** ($5 service charge will be added)
Bill-me option is good on US/Canada/
Mexico orders only; not good to jobbers,
wholesalers, or subscription agencies.

❏ **Signature** _____

❏ **Payment Enclosed: $** _____

❏ **PLEASE CHARGE TO MY CREDIT CARD:**

❏ Visa ❏ MasterCard ❏ AmEx ❏ Discover
❏ Diner's Club ❏ Eurocard ❏ JCB

Account # _____

Exp Date _____

Signature _____
(Prices in US dollars and subject to change without notice.)

PLEASE PRINT ALL INFORMATION OR ATTACH YOUR BUSINESS CARD

Name

Address

City   State/Province   Zip/Postal Code

Country

Tel   Fax

E-Mail

May we use your e-mail address for confirmations and other types of information? ❏Yes❏ No
We appreciate receiving your e-mail address. Haworth would like to e-mail special discount
offers to you, as a preferred customer. **We will never share, rent, or exchange your e-mail
address.** We regard such actions as an invasion of your privacy.

Order From Your Local Bookstore or Directly From
The Haworth Press, Inc.
10 Alice Street, Binghamton, New York 13904-1580 • USA
Call Our toll-free number (1-800-429-6784) / Outside US/Canada: (607) 722-5857
Fax: 1-800-895-0582 / Outside US/Canada: (607) 771-0012
E-Mail your order to us: Orders@haworthpress.com

Please Photocopy this form for your personal use.
www.HaworthPress.com

BOF04